GOOD DAY FOR A
PICNIC

GOOD DAY FOR A
PICNIC

❧

SIMPLE FOOD THAT TRAVELS WELL

Jeremy Jackson

𝒲𝓂
WILLIAM MORROW
An Imprint of HarperCollinsPublishers

HarperCollins books may be purchased for educational, business, or sales promotional
use. For information please write: Special Markets Department, HarperCollins
Publishers Inc., 10 East 53rd Street, New York, NY 10022.

FIRST EDITION

Designed by Renato Stanisic

Photograph on page iii © Ray Krantz/CORBIS

Photograph on page x © Underwood & Underwood/CORBIS

Photograph on page 19 © Minnesota Historical Society/CORBIS

Photograph on page 55 © Bettman/CORBIS

Photograph on page 95 © Bettman/CORBIS

Photograph on page 105 © Bettman/CORBIS

Photograph on page 155 © Genevieve Naylor/CORBIS

Printed on acid-free paper

Library of Congress Cataloging-in-Publication Data
Jackson, Jeremy, 1973–
    Good day for a picnic : simple food that travels well / Jeremy Jackson.
      p. cm.
    ISBN 0-06-072680-6
    1. Picnicking. I. Title.
TX823.J32   2005
641.5'78—dc22   2004054305

    05 06 07 WBC/RRD 10 9 8 7 6 5 4 3 2 1

For **KELLY**

CONTENTS

ACKNOWLEDGMENTS

As usual, I owe my editor, Harriet Bell, a big thank-you. She pushed me toward a larger project and kept me on track with just the right amount of guidance. I'm not quite sure how someone like me found an editor like her.

I'm a fan of Laura Calder's book *French Food at Home*, and when she volunteered to donate a few recipes to my picnic project, I was overjoyed. This book is better for her contributions, and I look forward to her next project.

I thank my friend Sorayah for inspirational lemonade ideas and "white trash champagne," which spurred me to try the German drink radler (page 22).

Mom and Dad, thanks for the freezer, the wonderful roadside, streamside, hilltop, and backyard picnics of the past, present, and future, and for raising us so that we knew what fresh, wholesome food tasted like and where it came from.

Claudia Roden wrote a fantastic picnic book more than twenty years ago, one which I treasure. She graciously allowed me to reprint one of her recipes here.

Finally, I bow to my girlfriend, Kelly. She invented a few of the recipes in this book, inspired several more, washed about half the dishes, and ate everything, even the failures.

Introduction

GORGING OUTDOORS

❧

I tried this thing the other day, this experiment. (Or, as my nephew would have called it when he was four, a "conspirament.") First, I arranged a modest assortment of appetizing foodstuffs on my kitchen counter. Then I stood in front of this small smorgasbord, if you will, wearing casual attire and with my hair still slightly askew from having slept on it the wrong way. (That's right, it was lunchtime and I hadn't combed my hair. But I *am* a writer, after all.) And then I smacked my lips, rubbed my hands together gleefully, and began.

I picked up a slice of orange. It was a colorful and floral wedge of citrus. I ate it and it was good and a bead of orange juice ran down my forearm and dripped off my elbow. Then I picked up another slice of orange and—pay attention here—*stepped outside and strode three paces away from the door*. There, in the warm autumn sunlight of my side yard, I ate the second orange slice. Again, the orange was good and a bead of juice ran down my forearm, etc. Then I asked myself a question. Did the second orange slice taste better than the first? In other words, does food taste better outside? Well, does it?

Picnics used to be the norm. Really. Think about it. Didn't our ancestors all eat outdoors? I don't mean our great-great-grandparents. I mean our biological ancestors—monkeys and whatnot—nibbling on berries. Or, to look at it another way, didn't Adam and Eve enjoy the fruits of Eden outdoors? When God booted them out of the garden, I think it's fair to summarize his message to them in this way: "All right, guys. Picnic's over."

Time, though, as it is wont to do, trudged onward. And someone discovered that caves were nice to sleep in. And someone invented architecture. And the next thing you know, some visionary was saying, "Hey, I got an idea: let's eat *inside*." Thus ended the first great age of picnics.

This isn't to say that people stopped eating outside. Think of the shepherds eating in the mountains and pastures for thousands of years in the Middle East, in North Africa, in Europe. Think of the caravans on the Silk Road, the native hunters in the dark forests of North America, the pilgrims trekking toward Canterbury or Mecca, the soldiers of countless kings and emperors and lords, the slaves building the pyramids, tilling the fields, clearing the land. Didn't all these millions of anonymous people eat outside frequently, if not daily? The Bible has all kinds of outdoor consumption going on. Just consider the Jews on their long journey from Egypt to Israel. Weren't they sort of picnicking the whole way? (Or would it be more accurately described as mobile noshing?)

But as I often say, eating outdoors does not a picnic make. So when was the modern idea of a picnic born? Nearly all the outdoor eating described above was done either out of necessity or convenience, though obviously it is at least partially related to today's picnic. But I wanted to know when the idea of a leisurely, slightly festive, possibly intimate outdoor meal was conceived. Perhaps the seasonal religious feasts and festivals of people all across the globe should be mentioned. But even more significant are the pursuits of the privileged classes. These were the people who had the luxury of dining inside all the time if they wanted to, which meant they could dine outside when they *felt* like it. The Frenchman Gaston de Foix described an outdoor hunting feast in 1387. And Jean Froissart, the French chronicler and poet, wrote this passage around the same time:

> Clear and fresh was the morn, and we came to a thorn-bush all white with blossom; lance-high it stood, with fair green shade beneath. Then said one, "Lo! a place made for our pleasant repose; here let us break our fast!" Then with one accord we brought forth the meats—pasties, hams, wines and bakemeats, and venison packed in heath. There was my lady ruler of the feast; and then it pleased her to say for the comfort of my martyrdom, that she retained me for her own; whereat my heart opened a fathom wide.

When I read this, I was so pleased I screamed like a little girl and nearly got myself kicked out of the library. What this passage showed was not only a *pleasure outing*, but a *romantic* pleasure outing. This indeed was a picnic. If I had had a big red stamp that read "PICNIC," I would have branded this passage right there in the library. Of course, our modern idea of romantic love and courtship was created in large part by writers like Froissart, Petrarch, and Dante in the thirteenth and fourteenth centuries, and therefore it isn't surprising that Froissart described one of the first romantic picnics, or that the French were doing it first.

We can also blame the French for giving picnics a name. *Pique-nique* is a simple compound word that appeared in France in the late 1600s. *Picorer* means to pick or peck at something. *Nique* is something of little value, some trifle. And the French were good at it. By the 1740s, the word had crossed over into English—perhaps via the German *picknick*—though to be fair, Londoners had been dining in outdoor pleasure gardens for decades already.

One of the most famous English picnic institutions, founded in 1800, was the Picnic Society, a group of stylish Londoners who met periodically to dine together. Each member brought a preassigned dish or beverage, which to me makes it sound as though the Picnic Society was really just a fancy potluck club, especially when you consider the fact that the Picnic Society actually met and dined *indoors* (in the Pantheon on Oxford Street, to be precise).

An indoor picnic? Good grief. The fashionable London imitation of the French *fête champêtre*—the garden party—was held indoors, too. Leave it to nineteenth-century Englishmen to kind of suck the fun out of any decent Continental idea. Ah, but the Enlightenment was over and the Romantic Movement was under way and England and much of Europe was changing. The days of indoor picnics were numbered! The Romantics, well, romanticized the landscape and sought to engage it directly. In other words, they got a lot of fresh air, and they ate outside while they were doing it. The Wordsworths had boating picnics. John Ruskin had an actual boat for picnicking. Picnicking was featured in popular novels by Jane Austen and Charles Dickens, just to name two. And you can hardly find a Victorian cookbook that doesn't include recipes for "tea in the garden." Queen Victoria herself enjoyed a good picnic.

Despite, or perhaps because of, their heroic efforts, the English did have a tendency to make even an outdoor picnic a bit stuffy and un-fun. *Mrs. Beeton's Book of Household Management,* a sort of home economics manual-to-end-all-manuals for the Victorian era, printed a list of "Not to be forgotten items for a PICNIC" in 1859. This list, admirable as it is in its intentions, does not deserve to go unmocked. Therefore, I present the entire list here, along with my commentary in brackets:

> A stick of horseradish [if you say so], bottles of mint-sauce [say what?], salad dressing [duh], vinegar [already got salad

dressing], and made mustard [fine], pepper [yes], salt [no, really?], good oil [as opposed to *bad* oil?], and pounded sugar [uh, a little help here?]. If it can be managed, take a little ice [no problem]. It is scarcely necessary to say that plates [yeah], tumblers [do you mean acrobats?], wine glasses [right], knifes [mm-hm], forks [yep], and spoons [sure thing] must not be forgotten, as also tea cups [are mugs okay?] and saucers [uh . . .], three or four teapots [you're kidding me], some lump sugar [the "pounded" sugar won't do?], and milk [all right], if this last-named article cannot be obtained in the neighborhood [hold on—do you mean we're supposed to get milk from any cows that happen to wander by?]. Take three corkscrews [why not four?]. Beverages—three dozen quart bottles of ale [!], packed in hampers; ginger-beer [ginger ale?], soda-water [club soda?], and lemonade [absolutely], of each two dozen bottles; six bottles of sherry [no thanks], six bottles of claret [the guy at the wine store looked at me funny when I said "claret"], champagne at discretion [thanks for allowing me to use my own judgment], and any other light wine [Thunderbird? Mad Dog 20/20?] that may be preferred, and two bottles of brandy [or let's just say *zero* bottles of brandy].

At the end of the day, the English did a pretty good job of popularizing the picnic. And thanks to their massive global domination scheme, they also introduced Europeanized picnic ideas basically everywhere. Including, of course, America.

While the English were busy waxing poetic about the landscape and tromping gleefully down mossy paths in the Lake Country, Americans were busy just trying to eke a living from the landscape. Americans were a breed of outdoorsmen by necessity, and therefore they ate outdoors an awful lot and didn't load such meals down with English frippery or formality. A cold corn pone and some salt pork eaten on horseback wouldn't have been called a picnic. This isn't to say that such a meal wasn't *enjoyed*, even in a country famous for its work ethic and suspicion of all things pleasurable. But even Cotton Mather, the famously tyrannical Puritan minister of colonial Massachusetts, was known to be a fisherman; and if he was a fisherman, doesn't that mean he probably ate a simple fisherman's meal on the stream bank or lakeshore? Wasn't that a picnic? Didn't he enjoy it?

Yes, yes, and yes.

The Puritans had their heyday long before *picnic* was even an English word, but they weren't the joy-haters we've pigeonholed them as. Bruce Daniels's book *Puritans at Play* details the many forms of recreation the Puritans enjoyed, including eating outdoors after communal workdays like house-raisings and harvestings. He also mentions the absolutely charming early American tradition of allowing the teenaged girls to abscond on an entire day of berry picking. And I think it's fair to assume that the girls packed simple lunches to be enjoyed out in the berry patch, along with some fresh, sun-warmed berries, of course. Daniels says that these berrying parties were "widely held everywhere in the seventeenth century," but later became more of a rural or small-town tradition.

Many of the American meals that prefigured picnics were communal. Barn raisings, cornhuskings, sheepshearings, and other such rural work meetings were frequently followed by dances and outdoor meals. One of the first things a western settler would do after claiming a piece of forested land was to call together his neighbors to help him clear the trees. People would come from far and wide for one of these "log rollings," as Foster Rhea Dulles details in *A History of Recreation*. The reward for all the hard work was a barbecue. The dinner after the log-rollings, Dulles writes, "was a gargantuan feast: a barbecued beef or hog roasted in a deep hole lined with hot stones; quantities of buffalo steaks, venison, baked 'possum or wild turkey; and always hominy, corn dodgers, and wheatcakes fried up in bear's oil."

Now that's good eatin'.

The New England clambake was another uniquely American out-door feast, which Kathy Neustadt chronicles beautifully in her book *Clambake*. The word *clambake* was first documented sometime between 1825 and 1840, and as the nineteenth century progressed, clambakes be-came wildly popular commercial ventures, and there were restaurants that specialized in hosting huge clambakes.

Americans liked to live large, especially in the Midwest and on the plains. Dulles mentions that two thousand people gathered for a Fourth of July barbecue and dance at Brownsville, Nebraska, in the mid-1800s. That's remarkable considering how widely scattered the settlers were in that territory at that time. At Blue Springs, Nebraska, Dulles notes, a "special committee caught one thousand pounds of catfish" for a simi-lar "frolic." That's the kind of committee I'd like to volunteer for. Nineteenth-century holidays and parades and reunions were nearly al-ways paired with huge outdoor feasts or barbecues. In the latter part of the century, Grange picnics would draw people from as far as a hundred miles away. All these large gatherings were rare excuses for people who spent much of their lives on isolated farms to come together and enjoy company and good food. The more densely populated East Coast—where even the farmers lived close to each other in townships—didn't really need such events.

Of course, smaller—and often more fashionable—picnics were hap-pening across the country, too. Colonial New York City supported a leisure class that was informed by the styles of London. According to Dulles, this set would ride out of the city and attend fashionable picnics on the East River. By the mid-nineteenth century, a wider class of New Yorkers was enjoying eating and socializing in outdoor gardens. "In New York's City Hall Park," writes Dulles, "scores of booths . . . [served] roast pig and spruce beer, lemonade and boiled eggs, lobsters and mint juleps, myriads of pies and cakes." Around the same time, wealthy southern landholders were holding "fashionable picnics." And Englishwoman Frances Trollope's famously caustic *Domestic Manners of the Americans,* published in 1832, includes a mention of people "eating strawberries and cream in a pretty garden" outside of Cincinnati.

One reason the nineteenth century saw the rise of the picnic in America was the development of local, state, and federal public parks. Small towns in the Midwest nearly all included a small public park— often right at the center of town surrounding the courthouse. These centralized parks frequently hosted dances, bands, socials, and picnics. After New York's Central Park was completed in the late 1850s, other cities, both large and small, began to follow suit. The availability of public parklands near at hand brought out all classes of people to picnic, especially in the cities, where the parks were a blessed refuge from the overcrowding, pollution, and general ugliness of city life. Cities also were populated more and more with European immigrants who brought with them their Continental traditions, which were more sensual and joy-seeking than the influences of the earlier immigrants such as the Puritans, Quakers, and Dutch Calvinists.

When I think of the American picnic since 1900, I get dizzy. It's fair to say that I get dizzy easily, though. But the reason I get dizzy in this instance is that the various forms and functions of the picnic in the twentieth and twenty-first centuries are legion.

At the start of the twentieth century, small-town, agrarian traditions were still widespread. Fourth of July picnics were common. In rural communities, a picnic day would be advertised in the local newspaper and people would drive their families out to the appointed field when the day came. Girls and women would go on berrying days.

My maternal grandmother and her siblings, growing up in the backwoods of the Missouri Ozarks in the 1910s and '20s, walked a couple miles to the one-room schoolhouse in Barren Hollow each day, and they carried their lunches with them in old lard pails. They usually had fresh biscuits in their lunches. If they were lucky, the biscuits had a dollop of sorghum molasses in them, or, better yet, they had been split, dipped in warm bacon drippings, sprinkled with sugar, and then put back together. (See Cinnamon-Buttered Split Biscuits, page 203; my great-uncle Rodger remembers tripping once and watching his biscuit fly out of his pail and roll down the hill.) Frequently the lunch pails contained hard-boiled eggs, along with a little pinch of salt folded neatly in a waxed paper packet. Often they had baked sweet potatoes, or apples that had been buried in the ground for months to preserve them. At lunchtime when the weather was warm, the children could eat outside. Imagine that: picnicking almost every day.

The urbanization and industrialization of America changed the way we picnic. Barn raisings and cornhuskings were replaced by professional builders and farm machinery. But picnics didn't disappear. They just found a new home. The twentieth century saw, for example, the rise of the company picnic. Originally, these picnics focused on games just as much as food. "Eating out of doors is fun," wrote Clark Fredrickson in *The Picnic Book* in 1942, "but without games or entertainment it won't be a picnic." Fredrickson's ideas for games include a strange scavenger hunt where everyone's given a long list of different attendees to locate and collect signatures from, such as "the woman who has the most buttons on her dress," "a Scotchman," and "a child attending the picnic who has four grandparents living." Doesn't this just amount to a novel form of harassment? "Hey, kid: are any of your grandparents dead?"

"Excuse me, ma'am, may I count your buttons?" There's even a whole section of the book devoted to "stalking games." And the ideas for themed picnics include "Let's Turn Hobo!" "Gypsy Jamboree," and "Indian Pow Wow." That's right, let's have fun by imitating people less fortunate than us. The few recipes in the book have titles like "Dog-With-a-Stick-in-His-Mouth."

A decade later, in the same vein, *The Complete Picnic Book*, by John E. Shallcross (that's right, *the* John E. Shallcross, Picnic Director for the City of Cleveland), has more than 100 pages devoted to games, and only twelve pages of recipes. His idea of a good sandwich was "Tongue, Swiss cheese, Bermuda onion, hard-boiled egg slices, topped off with chopped mustard pickle." His games are equally suspect. How about a round of "Drink and Run," anyone? Or how 'bout let's play "Chef Boxing," "Windbag," or "Hobble Kick"? "The more nonsensical the game," Shallcross writes, "the better."

Of course, these books—and the culture of the company picnic in general—are easy to make fun of now, but they do show how the new large companies in the midcentury were using picnics, which had long been centered around families and small towns, to create a sense of community and cohesiveness and belonging within their corporate culture.

The fund-raising picnic also thrived in the twentieth century. Think of the church picnics, the political steak fry, the fish fry hosted by the Lion's Club or some other civic group, the fall carnival thrown by the parochial schools, the Cub Scout weenie roast. Many of these events have become community traditions.

Smaller, personal picnics endure, too. A nice day in Manhattan brings office-dwellers out for sidewalk picnics. Families celebrate spring with simple backyard dining. Day hikers eat packed lunches on mountain peaks from Maine to Georgia. Couples pack baskets of food for long drives during leaf season. Family reunions burden tables with potato salads, pies, sandwiches. People dine on the deck as the sun sets. Farmers get off the tractor and sit in the shade of the trees and unpack small coolers of food. Winter revelers drink cocoa in front of a midnight bonfire.

This book is for all of them.

So anyway, I ate my whole lunch that way. I would take a bite of my sandwich inside. Chew, swallow. Then I would walk outside and take other bite. I ate one cookie inside, one outside. I even, believe it or not, ate one cookie standing on the threshold—half inside, half outside. Admittedly, it was a silly experiment, and an entirely unscientific one—one that anyone who has ever been on a picnic or two knew the answer to anyway. Yes, food tastes better outside. All food is a product of the sun, after all, and maybe that's the reason it's not surprising food tastes better under its benevolent warmth. A couple hundred years ago, the French gastronome Brillat-Savarin said it well:

> Seating themselves on the green sward they eat while the corks fly and there is talk, laughter, and merriment, and perfect freedom, for the universe is their drawing room and the sun their lamp. Besides, they have appetite, nature's special gift, which lends to such a meal a vivacity unknown indoors, however beautiful the surroundings.

And it's not just the appetite that is blessed by the outdoors. I propose that it's more than that. I propose that all the senses come alive outside, not just taste. Everything's just a little bit better.

One summer five years ago, while I was high up in the Sangre de Cristo mountains of New Mexico, fly-fishing for skittish little trout on a tiny creek, I stopped for lunch in a small meadow, laid my rod aside, and unwrapped my egg salad sandwich. It was a rudimentary picnic at best, but even a rudimentary picnic is a great picnic. And even a picnic enjoyed alone is a great picnic. And as I finished my lunch, I looked behind me and realized I was sitting at the edge of a patch of wild strawberries. There they were, little marble-size berries, just dangling there waiting for me. Perfect.

I think picnics have a way of stopping time and pulling the veil away from our eyes. Picnics connect us to our past and ground us in the present at the same time. That, in itself, is magic.

HOW TO THINK LIKE A PICNIC: A GUIDE

WHAT THIS BOOK CAN DO FOR YOU

No book could hope to encompass all outdoor eating. Therefore, I've limited my focus. I think that it's fair to say that in recent decades, barbecuing and grilling have taken on a robust and happy life of their own—with their own master cooks and cookbooks, gadgets and cults. The same goes for tailgating and campfire cooking. In this book, I've decided to write about picnics that require no grills and no cooking at the picnic site. In other words, all the work is done beforehand and the picnic itself is pure pleasure.

Also, I've decided to focus on simple, straightforward picnic fare. Somehow, straightforward and rustic food just works best outside, and I think it helps make a picnic more accessible to everyone. Picnic food, I think, should be timeless, not concerned with fads or fashions. For a picnic, I like to serve food that my grandparents and great-grandparents would have enjoyed and not have been puzzled by. But I also imagine that the same simple food will be enjoyed just as much many years from now, when my grandchildren encounter it. That is the kind of food I have put in this book. Of course, such food is satisfying and enjoyable no matter where it is served, so I hope readers will also utilize this book for their nonpicnic meals.

Picnics shouldn't be hard to prepare or complex, and that's another reason I've kept the recipes simple here. Also, you don't have to make *everything* on your picnic. Pick out one or two recipes from this book, make them, then buy some good bread and cheese and fruit and you're done. I'm a big fan of the "walk in, walk out" picnic. I walk into a good grocery store or deli or sandwich shop, and I walk out with a picnic. Don't let anyone tell you that that's cheating. It's not.

Though most of the recipes in this book are relatively quick and easy to prepare, I've also included twelve recipes that can be thrown together especially fast. I call them "Quick Pics" and put them at the ends of the chapters so that you can find them when you need them.

FOOD SAFETY

I don't want to sound like your Home Ec teacher, but whenever you talk about serving food hours or even days after it's made, food safety becomes an issue, especially when the food is going to be exposed to warm summer air. The threat of food poisoning is real.

Remember the two-hour rule. Eat food within two hours of when it's served. So two hours after that chilled salad comes out of the cooler, it's off limits. Same for hot foods and things that are best at room temperature. Be particularly careful with meat, seafood, poultry, eggs, and dairy products.

Keep cold things cold, hot things hot. This is a no-brainer, but it bears repeating. And keep the cold things separate from the hot things, of course. They can't both be transported in the same cooler. For cold things, don't leave your cooler in a hot car. Put your cooler in the shade at the picnic, and make sure there's plenty of ice inside. Ice melts, though, and can be messy. So put the ice in plastic bags or containers. Or freeze old plastic milk jugs filled with water and use them to keep your cooler cold. Don't have a cooler or need another one? A good cooler can be made with a strong cardboard box lined with blankets or newspaper.

HOW TO HAVE A PICNIC IN AN ANTIPICNIC WORLD

There are generally two kinds of picnic: the impromptu picnic and the planned picnic. They are both good.

For the impromptu picnic, you don't have a lot of preparation time. You may or may not have an hour or two in which to make a couple of quick recipes. If the weather is nice and you want to get away from it all, don't waste time fussing about the food. Do what works. If you want to encourage impromptu picnics, keep a "sudden picnic preparedness" basket or backpack in your pantry or closet. In the basket or backpack, have all the essentials prepacked: cutlery, a corkscrew, napkins, a blanket to sit on, etc. The more you have impromptu picnics, the better you get at it. So practice, practice, practice.

The planned picnic is a different creature altogether. Time is on your side, so you have the ability to organize and cook and think about whom to invite. Maybe you even want to send out formal invitations. Sounds good to me. For group picnics, you can call on your friends to bring food, too. Assign everyone a different dish, and that way you only have to bring one or two things. (Hey, I've got an idea: send out invitations *with a copy of this book* and let your guests pick a recipe!) Of course, with planned picnics, there are some variables that you can't predict. I'm speaking about the weather. Check the forecast, say a prayer, and have a rain site in mind.

Time is in short supply these days. So for many people, it's the biggest obstacle between them and a picnic. But remember that a picnic is a gift to yourself and your family and friends. You can find the time. After all, how much time do you waste sitting in your car each week, or watching horrible programs on television? And how about your lunch hour? Couldn't you have a nice little picnic with a friend or spouse during a sunny lunch hour? We all have to eat every day, and it doesn't take that much more time to make a picnic out of a meal.

So how do you have a picnic in an antipicnic world? You just do. It's up to you. And the world will be a better place with more picnics in it. That's a scientific fact.

WHAT TO BRING, AND NOT TO BRING

What to bring? How about a kite? Sunscreen. Sunglasses. An old blanket to sit on. Or old couch cushions. Lawn chairs. That warped Frisbee you keep forgetting to throw away. A ukelele. Sandals. A cowboy hat. A bouquet of wildflowers stuffed in a Mason jar. Some small pillows. Why not that bean bag chair that's leaking beans? Mr. Biggety (your dog). A croquet set. Anything NERF. A paperback book with a broken spine. Fingernail polish in the brightest possible color. A little table with sawed-down legs. Moist hand towels, like you're eating in a Japanese restaurant. Your box of watercolors and a tablet of paper. Several marbles, with which to invent a new game. A pocketknife. Gum. A string of big Christmas lights (even though there won't be an outlet). And food, food, food . . .

This is not the kind of book where I am going to give you a checklist of every necessary picnic item. I trust you to remember the napkins, silverware, bug spray, etc. For the few recipes that require special serving tools, I've included packing reminders on the recipe page. But be prepared for the fact that *you will forget to bring something*. That's okay. You'll bring it next time. In the meantime, have fun trying to cut up a watermelon with a penknife.

As for things *not* to bring, well, first off, I don't think cell phones should be allowed at a picnic. Nor any portable electronic device. The only exception I can think of is maybe a tiny transistor radio to play some tinny AM tunes. Call me old-fashioned, but I just think electronics are contrary to the picnic atmosphere. Picnics are a time to get away from the television and Internet and all that stuff. Such things are part of the antipicnic world. I even think that cameras don't belong at a picnic (though I'm not going to officially ban them). I personally don't want to be photographed while trying to fit a huge sandwich in my mouth, or when I fall asleep with flies buzzing around my mouth. And cameras and camcorders have a way of distracting us from the moment and making everyone a little bit self-conscious. So, preferably, no cameras. And while I'm thinking of it, how about no watches? That's right: leave your watch at home and tell your time by the sun. That's liberation. That's what I'm talking about.

WHEN TO HAVE A PICNIC

Sometime this week.

WHERE

Look for grassy open spaces. Look for shade. Look for streams and parks and benches by old bridges. Backyards with lopsided picnic tables. Willow trees. Courtyards with grass sprouting between the paving stones. Anyplace in sight of goldfish. The lawn behind the state capitol. All the usual suspects.

Or:

How about a small airport? You can park pretty close to the runway and sit on the trunk of your car and watch someone practice landing in an old yellow de Haviland.

Orchards. Many will let you picnic right there, under the trees. What could be better on a warm afternoon in early autumn?

Bike trails, greenways, and pedestrian paths have proliferated in my lifetime, and they can be terrific little getaways, even in busy cities. They often follow rivers.

Nothing builds an appetite like a long hike, and usually the scenery can't be beat. The best part is that your backpack is a lot lighter after lunch.

Organize a berrying expedition, just like in the old days. Of course, to do this, you have to know where the berries are, and have permission to get to them and pick them.

The beach, of course, of course.

A treehouse? I like it.

Is there such a thing as a winter picnic? Indoors by the fireplace? Or in a tent on the living room floor? Yes, yes, yes.

Some minor league ballparks let you bring food in.

Finally: canoe, sailboat, motorboat, raft, pontoon boat, kayak, yacht. Ship or shore. Noon or night.

DRINKS, STARTERS, AND SMALL BITES

CRÈME DE CASSIS COCKTAIL

✳

This bubbly, low-alcohol berry concoction is a summery drink if ever there was one. It's a fantastic aperitif, and goes well with many picnic foods.

MAKES 1 SERVING

½ cup club soda

1½ teaspoons crème de cassis, or to taste

In a small glass, pour the club soda over ice, then stir in the crème de cassis and serve.

PIMM'S

✳

Yes, I know the label on the venerable English spirit claims that its formula is "a closely guarded secret known only to six people," but I don't give a flying fruitcake what's in it. It's good—junipery and fruity and spicy—and it makes one of the best summer cocktails around. It's a real thirst quencher; but be warned that it's stronger than it tastes. And how could you not love a cocktail with a cucumber garnish?

By all means, vary the amounts of lemonade and ginger ale here to suit your taste. Some people like a few mashed mint leaves mixed in. And notice that it's an easy recipe to scale up or down, even if you're a little sloshed.

MAKES 4 SERVINGS

1 cup Pimm's No. 1

1 cup strong lemonade (made with the juice of 2 lemons, about 1 tablespoon sugar, and enough water to make 1 cup)

1 cup ginger ale or lemon-lime soda

Lemon slices

Lime slices

Cucumber slices

Fresh mint, optional

In a pitcher, stir together the Pimm's, lemonade, ginger ale, and a few slices of lemon, lime, and cucumber. (At this point, you can pour it into a container with a lid and transport the drink to the picnic.) Pour over ice in tall glasses. Garnish each glass with one slice each of lemon, lime, and cucumber. Add a few crushed mint leaves, if desired.

RADLER

✳

This probably doesn't even qualify as a recipe, I'll admit, but it's so smackingly refreshing and summerlicious it deserves a whole page of its own. The story goes like this: in 1922, an innkeeper in Bavaria didn't have enough beer to accommodate the bicyclists and other guests, so he cut the beer with lemon-lime soda and it was a hit. He named it "radler," which means "cyclist."

So, is this the German equivalent of Gatorade? Kinda. The beer tempers the sweetness of the soda, and the soda mellows the bitterness of the beer, and the result is fruity and light tasting and has half the alcohol of beer. In my experience, though, it's so good I drink twice what I should, so be warned. I like it with pale American beer (full honesty moment: Busch Light), but by all means, experiment with different brews.

MAKES 2 SERVINGS

12-ounce can cold lemon-lime soda

12-ounce can cold beer

Pour equal amounts of the soda into the bottoms of 2 large glasses, then top with equal amounts of beer. No stirring required.

CHAMPAGNE PUNCH #5

✳

I n other words, I developed, mixed, and drank four other champagne punches before I was convinced I had found the perfect one. By that point, as you can imagine, I was a little drunk, so I wondered if my judgment was impaired, but testing this punch later proved that it was a clear winner. What I liked about it is that all its components merged and it became something completely new and balanced and summerlicious.

It's a spectacularly red punch, with pretty slices of oranges bobbling along. Serve it in a pitcher, jug, punch bowl, goldfish bowl, bucket . . . whatever works. It's easy to transport to a picnic because the champagne is left unopened until the last moment, thus preserving the bubbles.

Modestly priced sparkling wine performs very well here. Save the good stuff for another time.

MAKES ABOUT 6 SMALL SERVINGS OR 4 LARGE SERVINGS

2 cups fresh or thawed frozen raspberries

2 cups ginger ale

¾ cup pineapple juice

2 oranges, cut into thin rounds

750 ml bottle cold champagne or sparkling wine

At least a few hours before the picnic, make the "prepunch." With your fingers or the back of a spoon, mash the raspberries through a medium-mesh sieve until just the seeds remain. Combine the raspberry pulp with the ginger ale, pineapple juice, and orange rounds. Chill this mixture for at least 3 hours or for up to 2 days.

Immediately before serving, combine the cold raspberry mixture with the champagne.

GINGER ICED TEA

✴

Spicy but not peppery. Refreshing but subtle. This do-all summer-time thirst quencher can be served in small portions as an aperitif or in big tumblers during a meal. It's also good hot. Or try it as a mix-in with your favorite iced tea.

MAKES ABOUT 6 SERVINGS

6-inch-long piece peeled fresh ginger

Light brown sugar, honey, or sugar to taste

Slice the ginger into thin rounds and cover it with 8 cups boiling water. Steep for 20 minutes, then strain. Let it cool before pouring it over ice, or chill it in the fridge and it doesn't even need ice.

LEMONADE AND VARIATIONS

✳

It's not quite summer without it, is it? So don't settle for that instant stuff or pay six dollars for a half gallon of bottled mediocrity. Go for the real deal. It only takes a couple of minutes to make.

This is just a set of guidelines, really. Everyone has their own style of lemonade, so by all means add more or less lemon juice, sugar, etc. Substitute lime juice. Use honey as a sweetener. Go crazy.

Remember, room-temperature lemons produce more juice. I like to leave the lemon pulp in, but feel free to strain it out. Also remember that different lemons produce different amounts of juice. Those huge, hard lemons in the supermarket often aren't very juicy. Soft (but not too soft) lemons contain more juice.

With leftover lemonade, try making Lemonade Syrup (page 202).

MAKES ABOUT 6 SERVINGS

Juice of 8 lemons

¾ cup sugar, or to taste

In a serving pitcher, stir the lemon juice and sugar with 6 or 7 cups of water until the sugar is dissolved. Taste and adjust the sweetness. Serve over ice or chill. Lemonade keeps respectably well in the fridge.

EASY LEMONADE ADDITIONS

✳ *Rose water.* About ¾ teaspoon or more per pitcher adds a fabulous floral note that will keep your guests guessing. Be careful not to add too much: it can be a tad medicinal.

✳ *Angostura aromatic bitters.* That's right, raid the liquor closet and put several dashes, to taste, right into the lemonade.

It tints the lemonade a slight pinkish brown, and the spicy elusiveness makes the lemonade particularly refreshing. When I make Chef's Lemonade (below) I almost always add a couple of dashes of bitters.

✳ *Mint.* A classic. Crush several leaves between your palms and let them steep in the lemonade. The longer they're in there, the more flavor they'll impart.

CHEF'S LEMONADE

✳

Many recipes call for only a tablespoon or so of lemon (or lime) juice, which means that I'm forever putting halves of lemons back in the fridge, where they often go bad before they're used. So recently, whenever I'm in the kitchen cooking and the recipe spawns half a lemon, instead of sending it to a cold and moldy demise I squeeze it immediately—by hand—right into a 10-ounce tumbler, scooping out the seeds (or not), adding water, stirring in sugar to taste (a couple of teaspoons?), and then drinking the fresh lemonade while I continue cooking. Sometimes I add two dashes of Angostura bitters. What could be better in a hot kitchen?

RASPBERRY LEMONADE

✳

This summer brew packs a visual wallop that makes plain old pink lemonade look watered down. I don't think I've ever seen a drink that looked quite so gorgeous, especially in sunlight. Of course, this isn't a beauty contest, so how does it taste? Even better than its looks. There's really no trick to it at all, you can make it ahead, and you can substitute blackberries if you like. 'Nuff said.

MAKES ABOUT 6 SERVINGS

2 cups (about 10 ounces) raspberries, rinsed

Juice of 4 lemons

1/2 cup sugar, or to taste

Mash the raspberries in a medium-mesh strainer with the back of a spoon, until all the pulp has passed through, leaving the seeds. Combine the raspberry pulp with 8 cups water and the remaining ingredients. Stir until the sugar is dissolved. Add more sugar or lemon juice, if desired.

Serve immediately or chill for up to 2 days. Stir before serving.

JORDANIAN LEMONADE

✳

My friend Sorayah, who lived for five years in Jordan, told me that this is how they make lemonade there, so I gave it a try and I adored it. The orange juice adds a certain roundness and warmth that you don't find in regular lemonade.

MAKES ABOUT 6 SERVINGS

Juice of 8 lemons

Juice of 2 oranges

¾ cups sugar, or more to taste

A couple dozen small fresh mint leaves, lightly crushed

Combine all the ingredients with 6 or more cups water and stir until the sugar is dissolved. Taste for sweetness, then serve immediately or chill.

STRAWBERRY-WATERMELON SMOOTHIE

✳

When the berries and melons are good, there's really no reason to fuss around and try to improve their flavor. Serve portions of this essence of summer before or after a meal.

MAKES ABOUT 6 SERVINGS

6 cups watermelon chunks

2 cups sliced strawberries (about 1 pint)

2 tablespoons sour cream

To strain the seeds out of the watermelon chunks, press them through a food mill or sieve. (Or use a seedless melon. Or just cut out the parts of the watermelon with no seeds.) Working in two batches, combine all the ingredients in a blender with ½ cup water and blend until smooth. Combine the batches. Serve cold the same day.

SEKANJABIN
(VINEGAR SYRUP DRINK)

✳

I'd never heard of sekanjabin until recently, and I wasn't all that excited by the ingredients list. Vinegar? In a drink? That seemed wacky. But sekanjabin has been popular in the Middle East for more than a thousand years, and that kind of popularity can't be a fluke. So I tried it. And adored it.

It's a sweet-and-sour drink, and it *doesn't* taste like vinegar. (Remember vinegar pie?) It's floral and spicy. And it's very refreshing. It comes from the desert, after all. The concentrated syrup keeps almost indefinitely at room temperature or refrigerated. One batch of syrup will make dozens of glasses of thirst quencher. Or a few pitchers.

MAKES ENOUGH FOR MANY SERVINGS

1 cup sugar

¼ cup white wine or red wine vinegar

1 fresh mint sprig, or to taste

In a small nonreactive pan, bring the sugar, white wine vinegar, and ⅓ cup water to a simmer over medium heat, stirring occasionally to dissolve the sugar. Lower the heat and simmer gently until the mixture is a very thin syrup, about 30 minutes. Remove it from the heat and add the mint. When the syrup has cooled completely, remove the mint and pour it into a small jar for storage.

For an individual serving, a rough guideline is to put about a finger's width of syrup in the bottom of a glass, then add ice and water and stir.

The Wine Page

Vinho Verde. Perhaps the perfect picnic wine. Literally "green wine," these inexpensive white wines (reds are also made, but rarely exported) from northern Portugal are peppery, nicely acidic, low in alcohol, and slightly effervescent. Drink vinho verde young and cold. Expect to pay $6 to $12.

Pinot Grigio. Everyone seems to adore this outgoing white—U.S. sales have skyrocketed in recent years. The same grape is called Pinot Gris in France and in some other parts of the world. Expect to pay $7 to $20.

Rosé. Forget the syrupy-sweet pink supermarket wine that has given rosé a bad name. (Not that you shouldn't guzzle white zinfandel if that's what floats your boat.) Instead, look for the dry and off-dry blushing beauties like Tavel from France—perhaps the most famous rosé of all—or a Cabernet Sauvignon rosé from South Africa. Choices abound here, prices are reasonable, and most rosés are supple, food friendly, and good chilled. Expect to pay $7 to $20.

Beaujolais Nouveau. The quintessential quaffing wine. Grapey and joyful and not too tannic. As it's best drunk young, picnickers are put in a bit of a quandary, since the fresh vintage of Beaujolais is released in November of each year—not exactly picnic weather. The good news is that the wine will still be lip-smacking good by the time picnic season rolls around. Expect to pay $8 to $18.

Picpoul de Pinet. *Picpoul* means "lip stinger" and that gives you a pretty good idea of this delicious wine's character. Fret not, though: the wine's acidity is well balanced by lush fruit and just a touch of natural carbonation. It's not a complex wine, but straightforward quaffing wine that tastes great when drunk in sunlight and plays well with all kinds of food. Expect to pay $6 to $12.

Riesling. Why the great white grape of Germany has never taken off in America is beyond me. I'd take a glass of Riesling over Chardonnay any day. Fragrant, often with just a touch of sweetness, bursting with peach flavor, Riesling is a go-to wine when you want an outdoor wine with integrity. That said, you don't have to be a wine snob to enjoy it: a good Riesling holds nothing back and offers itself to you in a straightforward but utterly charming way. Lovely Rieslings are made in Oregon, Washington, New York, and Australia, but Germany and France produce the best. Expect to pay $8 to $30.

Alsatian whites. The prices are right, the quality is reliably good, and . . . well, I just love those slender green bottles. Varietals include Pinot Blanc, Riesling, Pinot Gris, and Gewürztraminer. Half bottles are easy to find. Expect to pay $8 to $24.

Sparkling wines. Champagne is a picnic classic, and with good reason. It's bubbly, cold, and festive. The Spanish sparklers are a real bargain, as are many American bottlings. And keep an eye peeled for those little 187 ml bottles of champagne—they're cute and practical. Expect to pay $9 to $50 (about $3 for 187 ml bottles).

BROWN SUGAR ALMONDS

✳

These are picnic-worthy not just because of their sugar-encrusted goodness, but because you can make them days ahead of time and serve them as soon as you arrive at the picnic site, before the rest of the food is unpacked. Hey, and if you serve them in the car on the way to the picnic, that's okay, too, though technically that's not a picnic. Admittedly, it's a smallish recipe, but there's a reason for that: the almonds are so good that people would fill up on them if given the chance. Feel free to double the amount.

For the best almonds, get them from a good natural foods store. Walnuts work well in this recipe, too.

MAKES ABOUT 6 SERVINGS
1 tablespoon unsalted butter

1 cup raw almonds

⅛ teaspoon salt

3 tablespoons light brown sugar

Spread a piece of aluminum foil or parchment paper on a work surface to cool the almonds on later.

Melt the butter in a medium skillet over medium-low heat. Add the nuts and cook, stirring frequently, until hot and sizzling very softly, 3 to 5 minutes.

Sprinkle the salt over the nuts. Push the sugar through a medium-mesh strainer, sprinkling it over the almonds, and continue cooking and stirring until the sugar is completely molten, about 10 minutes. It won't stick to the nuts much at this point.

Remove the pan from the heat and continue stirring until the sugar cools just enough that it coats the nuts. Pour the nuts onto the foil or parchment paper. Spread the nuts into a single layer and use a fork to separate them if you wish.

When the nuts are cool, they can be stored at room temperature in an airtight container for a few weeks.

BURNT SUGAR ALMONDS

✳ If you like the dark flavor of burnt sugar, follow the recipe above except let the nuts and sugar cook until the sugar is molten and dark, about 15 minutes. It may also smoke slightly.

CHERRY TOMATOES STUFFED WITH MINTED GOAT CHEESE

✳

I had a patch of dry, barren dirt on the hot west side of my house where nothing would grow. So I put in three mint plants, and next thing I knew I had a mint forest, which in my book is a very good thing.

These stuffed tomatoes achieve the three goals I wish all recipes could: simplicity, attractiveness, and, of course, fantastic taste. They pack a lot of flavor into bite-size morsels, perfect fare to whet your appetite. You can substitute herbs like cilantro or parsley for the mint. And the minted cheese makes a nice spread for crusty bread, too.

MAKES ABOUT 50 STUFFED TOMATO HALVES TO SERVE 6

½ cup goat cheese (about 4 ounces)

Milk

20 medium fresh mint leaves, finely chopped

Salt and freshly ground black pepper

1 pint cherry tomatoes

With a fork, mash the cheese in a bowl. Drizzle in a bit of milk and keep mashing and stirring until the mixture is smooth and spreadable—about like cream cheese. Stir in the mint leaves and salt and pepper to taste.

Wash and dry the tomatoes, then cut them in half. Scoop out the seeds with your fingers, then spoon bits of the cheese into the hollowed-out shells. Chill until serving.

WALNUT AND FETA MICRO-QUICHES

✳

Micro indeed: these two-bite wonders are baked in mini-muffin pans, but there's nothing small about their flavor. Feta cheese and walnuts are a classic pairing that really can't be improved on, but for something different you can leave out the feta and top the quiches with dollops of crème fraîche just before serving. Like many appetizers, these could make for a nice little lunchtime picnic if paired with a salad and some fruit. They're easy to pack and, like most quiches, good at any temperature.

MAKES 24 MICRO-QUICHES TO SERVE 4 TO 6

½ recipe Whole Wheat Quiche Pastry, chilled but not rolled out (page 133)

2 teaspoons extra virgin olive oil

½ cup finely chopped onion

1 tablespoon all-purpose flour

¼ plus ⅛ teaspoon salt

¼ teaspoon dried thyme

Freshly ground black pepper

½ cup whole milk

1 large egg

1 cup chopped walnuts

½ cup feta cheese, or more as needed

Roll the chilled pastry dough into a 14-inch-diameter circle and cut out twenty-four 2½-inch circles with a biscuit cutter or the rim of a small glass. Fit the circles into a nonstick mini-muffin baking pan. Chill until needed.

Preheat the oven to 375°F.

Heat the olive oil over medium heat, then add the onion and sauté until soft, 5 to 10 minutes. Remove the onion from the heat and stir in the flour, salt, thyme, and pepper.

Beat the milk and egg together, then stir into the onion mixture. Divide the onion mixture among the 24 quiche cups. There may be some left-over filling. Top the quiches with the walnuts.

Bake for 12 to 18 minutes, until the quiches are set and puffed. Top the hot quiches with crumbled feta cheese, then put them under the broiler just until the cheese is hot and soft.

Though best the day they're made, they can be refrigerated for a couple of days. For a picnic, serve them at room temperature. For dining at home—or a backyard picnic—they can be served hot or warm. They can be transported in the mini-muffin pan.

SWEET AND SOUR PEARL ONIONS

✳

No, they aren't going to change the world or show up on the covers of food magazines anytime soon, but, bottom line, *they disappear fast*. And that's what matters, isn't it? They're slick little buggers, though, so if you serve them as appetizers, be a pal and skewer them with toothpicks ahead of time. Do a double batch for a side dish.

SERVES 6 FOR APPETIZERS, 3 FOR A SIDE DISH

10 ounces white or yellow pearl onions

3 tablespoons extra virgin olive oil

3 tablespoons white wine or champagne vinegar

1 tablespoon balsamic vinegar

2 teaspoons light brown sugar

1 garlic clove, minced

½ teaspoon salt

Freshly ground black pepper

To peel the onions, drop them into boiling water, boil for 3 minutes, then drain. Clip both ends of the onions with a pair of kitchen shears, then squeeze toward the root end. The onions will pop right out of their skins.

In a medium skillet over medium heat, heat the olive oil, then sauté the onions, stirring often, until lightly browned, 5 to 10 minutes. Off the heat, add the remaining ingredients and just enough water so that the onions are floating. Simmer 3 to 5 minutes. They will be very tender by this point. Drain and let cool. Serve at room temperature or cold. They can be kept refrigerated for up to 3 days.

ROASTED GRAPES

✳

Maybe roasted grapes should be called "half raisins" ("graisins"?) since they're somewhere between fresh grapes and raisins. They have the caramelized sweetness of raisins with the juiciness and fresh taste of grapes. What more could you want? Well, how about ease of preparation and versatility? For example, plate them right alongside the salty richness of imported prosciutto and you've got antipasto that's about as good as it gets. But don't stop there. They're a natural pairing with Pine Nut Butter (page 40), for example. Or add the roasted grapes to salads, serve them with goat cheese and water crackers, top bruschetta with them, or dribble them onto slices of cake or good vanilla ice cream. What *can't* they do?

MAKES ABOUT 6 SMALL SERVINGS

1½ pounds red seedless grapes, washed

Red wine vinegar

Preheat the oven to 400°F. Line a baking sheet with parchment paper.

Remove the grapes from the stems and put them on the baking sheet. Sprinkle with just a little bit of red wine vinegar, then bake for 40 to 60 minutes—turning once—until they are soft and quite brown. Some grapes will be brown faster than others, but that's okay.

Remove the grapes from the parchment while they're still warm. The grapes can be refrigerated for a week. Serve them at room temperature.

PINE NUT BUTTER

✳

You gotta love a recipe with one ingredient. That's it. All the better to showcase the little nut with the big flavor. The fun, of course, comes when you start to combine the fresh nut butter with other things. It all makes you feel like a kid again.

You can make nut butter with any nut, of course. Blenders will work—with lots of scraping down—but the best tool is a stick blender (sometimes called an immersion blender). This is a small recipe, and I recommend keeping it that way. It's a rich appetizer, and one that's addictive.

MAKES ABOUT 6 SERVINGS

1 cup raw pine nuts

Toast the nuts in a dry skillet over medium heat, shaking frequently, just until they begin to sizzle very softly and show the first signs of light browning, 3 to 5 minutes. Let the nuts cool a bit, then process them with a stick blender until the mixture is about the same consistency as natural peanut butter. The nut butter can be stored at room temperature for a couple of days.

PINE NUT BUTTER PAIRINGS

✳ Pine nut butter with Roasted Grapes (page 39) on crackers or bread

✳ Pine nut butter with fresh goat cheese on crackers or bread

✳ Pine nut butter drizzled with honey on crackers or bread

✳ Fresh apple slices, carrot sticks, etc., dipped in pine nut butter

✳ Ants on a log? Spread pine nut butter inside small celery sticks and top them with Roasted Grapes (page 39).

FIG PÂTÉ

✳

Because of its shape, this unusual but happy-making fig thing is referred to lovingly in my house as a "fig log," and you're welcome to call it that, too. I've enjoyed it during many a midday meal standing at my kitchen counter with an assortment of other small edible things I could find, like goat cheese, cornichons, smoked trout, grapes, water crackers, and some wine or Crème de Cassis Cocktail (page 20). Why not make a whole picnic out of appetizers? Slice the log like a salami and eat it straight or on a cracker. It keeps forever.

MAKES ONE 6-INCH LOG TO SERVE 8

¼ cup hazelnuts

baking soda

1 teaspoon fennel seeds, or to taste

1¼ cups dried Black Mission figs, stemmed and halved

1 tablespoon brandy

1½ teaspoons balsamic vinegar

Freshly ground black pepper

To remove the skins from the hazelnuts without toasting them, bring some water and ½ teaspoon baking soda to boil in a small pot, boil the nuts for a few minutes, then drain the nuts and rub off their skins with a kitchen towel.

Toast the fennel seeds in a small skillet over medium heat just until they start to change color. Grind them in a spice grinder or clean coffee grinder.

Place the hazelnuts, figs, brandy, balsamic vinegar, and 1½ teaspoons water in the bowl of a food processor. Process until the mixture is a paste. Add the ground fennel and black pepper to taste.

Place the fig paste on a sheet of aluminum foil and shape it into a rough 6-inch log, then wrap it tightly in the foil, rolling to shape it into a perfect cylinder. Unwrap the foil and place the log—still on the foil—onto a baking sheet and bake at 200°F until the surface of the log dries out and hardens a little bit, 20 to 25 minutes. Let it cool.

Wrap the log securely in foil and keep it in a zipper-lock bag in the refrigerator for up to 2 months. Serve cold or at room temperature.

ZUCCHINI FRITTERS

✳

These Indian-inspired baby-pancake-like fritters pack a world of flavor in a small package. Still, they're not really complete until you dip them into the cool, fresh flavor of Cilantro Chutney (page 45). Though their texture is best when they're fresh, they're still commendably good hours later.

MAKES ABOUT 35 SMALL FRITTERS

12 ounces zucchini, about 2 medium zucchinis

½ cup cooked and mashed potato

1 large egg, slightly beaten

½ onion, diced

2 garlic cloves, minced

1 teaspoon ground cumin

½ teaspoon ground cardamom

¼ teaspoon turmeric

¼ teaspoon cayenne pepper

Pinch of cinnamon

Freshly ground black pepper

½ teaspoon salt, or to taste

Olive oil, for frying

Grate the zucchini, then stir it together with the remaining ingredients—except the olive oil—until the mixture is uniform.

Add enough olive oil to nearly cover the bottom of a large nonstick skillet. Heat the oil over medium heat. Drop tablespoon-size patties of the batter onto the oil and fry until nicely browned, about 5 minutes on each side. Drain the hot fritters on paper towels.

For a picnic, the fritters can be refrigerated for a day and served at room temperature. For dining at home, or a backyard picnic, the fritters are especially good while still warm.

CILANTRO CHUTNEY

✳

When my girlfriend and I eat at our favorite Indian restaurant, we always enjoy the cilantro chutney served as a dip with pakoras and samosas. We love the chutney so much we also put it over rice. This isn't the chunky, fruity kind of chutney, but more like a thin pesto sauce, and in addition to being a perfect dip for Zucchini Fritters (page 43), it's a good dip for raw vegetables, or even as a spread on bread.

MAKES 1 CUP

2 cups packed fresh cilantro

1/2 cup packed fresh mint

2 jalapeno peppers

4 teaspoons freshly squeezed lime juice

1 teaspoon ground cumin

1/2 teaspoon salt

Combine all the ingredients with 6 tablespoons water in the bowl of a blender. Blend, scraping the sides down occasionally, until a smooth sauce forms. (It may look impossible at first, but I find that by just running the blender for a few minutes without interruption the chutney nearly takes care of itself.)

Serve immediately or chill for up to 2 days.

GOUGÈRES WITH FONTINA AND CHIVES

✳

Them's shore are some durn fancy cheese puffs. If you've never had gougères before, I think the best way to describe them is as tiny, savory cream puffs. Without any cream filling, of course. French names and awkward descriptions aside, they're about as good as any food ever invented, period, and I can pop about twelve in my mouth while no one's looking. They're not hard to make, either.

MAKES ABOUT 80 SMALL PUFFS
4 tablespoons (½ stick) unsalted butter

½ teaspoon salt

Freshly ground black pepper

⅔ cup all-purpose flour

2 large eggs

¾ cup Fontina cheese, grated (about 3 ounces)

1 tablespoon chopped chives

Preheat the oven to 375°F. Line 2 large baking sheets with parchment paper.

In a medium saucepan, bring the butter, salt, pepper, and ⅔ cup water to a boil. Off the heat, add the flour, and stir vigorously until the mixture is smooth and comes away from the sides of the saucepan to make a big clump.

Return the saucepan to low heat and stir continuously for about a minute, or until a dry film forms on the bottom of the pan. Remove the pan from the heat again and let it cool for a few minutes.

Add one egg and stir quickly and patiently until it is completely incorporated, then add the other egg and stir until you have a smooth mixture. Stir in the cheese and chives.

With a pastry bag (or plastic zipper-lock bag with one corner cut off), squeeze ¾-inch blobs of the paste onto the parchment-lined baking sheets, spacing them about an inch apart. Bake the gougères until they are lightly browned and cooked through, about 25 minutes.

For a picnic, the gougères are best served at room temperature the same day they're made. Don't put warm gougères in an airtight container or they may get soggy. But once they've cooled, they can be stored a couple of days like this.

CROSTINI WITH PEACHES AND BLUE CHEESE

✳

The world-famous Maytag blue cheese comes from right here in Iowa, and I'm always looking for excuses to use it. I wasn't sure whether it would marry well with peaches, so when I developed this recipe I tried it with fromage blanc, too. Well, the blue cheese was the hands-down victor, and that's the end of the story. When peaches are in season, I could eat these crostini every day and not get tired of them.

MAKES 12 CROSTINI

12 thin slices baguette or similar bread

(stale bread is fine)

Olive oil, for brushing

3 to 4 ripe peaches

2 tablespoons balsamic vinegar

¾ to 1 cup blue cheese, crumbled

Freshly ground black pepper, optional

Brush the bread slices with just a bit of olive oil, then toast, bake, grill, or broil the bread until it's almost dry.

To peel the peaches, boil them for 30 seconds, then immediately transfer them to a bowl of ice water. The skin will come off easily. Slice the peaches into very small and thin pieces and combine them with the balsamic vinegar.

Preheat the broiler to low.

Arrange the bread on a baking sheet. Top the bread slices with the peaches and their juices. Put the crumbled cheese on top of the peaches, and add just a touch of black pepper, if desired.

Broil the crostini until the cheese is hot, soft, and just touched with brown. Serve at any temperature, preferably within a couple hours of being made.

CORNSOMMÉ

✳

hat's not a typo. Since consommé is a clear soup made with meat broth, I figured that this flavorful palate-opening starter soup made with corn should be called *corn*sommé. A lot of the flavor comes from simmering the corncobs in water, a.k.a. corncob broth. Serve it warm or cold in very small bowls. For great sweet corn, shop at farmer's markets in season.

MAKES ABOUT 6 SMALL SERVINGS

3 ears sweet corn, shucked and cleaned

1 shallot, chopped

2 or 3 fresh thyme sprigs

½ garlic clove, chopped

Salt and freshly ground black pepper

In a pot large enough to hold the corncobs, bring 4 cups water to a boil. Boil the corn on the cob for 3 minutes, covered, then remove and let cool. Leave the boiling liquid in the pot.

Cut the corn kernels from the cob, then scrape the cobs with the back edge of your knife to extract the "milk." Reserve the corn kernels and milk.

Put the bare corncobs back in the hot water, along with the shallot, thyme, garlic, and a bit of salt and pepper. Simmer the mixture for 15 minutes or so.

Pass the corn kernels and corncob broth through the fine screen of a food mill. Be patient, making sure all the juice is extracted from the corn. (For an even smoother soup, puree the corn and broth before straining.) Taste for salt and pepper.

For a picnic, transport the soup in a thermos or plastic pitcher with a lid so that it's easy to pour into individual bowls.

"QUICK PIC" APPETIZERS
AND SMALL BITES

✳

SMOKED OYSTERS WITH HORSERADISH YOGURT

Being from a landlocked state, I get a bit squeamish around shell-fish sometimes, but as soon as I tasted these simple morsels, I was a fan. Feel free to substitute smoked trout or salmon for the oysters.

Mix 2 parts plain yogurt to 1 part prepared horseradish (or to taste). Drain a tin of smoked oysters. At the picnic site, put one oyster on a water cracker and top with a small dollop of the horseradish yogurt. Repeat and enjoy.

SIMPLER SCOTCH EGGS

Quintessential picnic fare in England, the usual recipe for these substantial appetizers calls for coating an entire hard-boiled egg in sausage meat and bread crumbs and then deep-frying it. I prefer a simpler approach. Use whatever sausage you desire—from spicy chorizo to good old bratwurst.

Cut the casing from 4 to 5 ounces of sausage and mash the sausage with the back of a spoon to make it smooth and spreadable. Cut 6 hard-boiled eggs in half. Spread the sausage on the cut sides of the eggs, then press finely grated fresh bread crumbs onto the sausage.

Heat a very thin layer of olive oil in a nonstick skillet over medium heat. Fry the eggs sausage side down until the sausage is cooked and the bread crumbs are browned, about 5 minutes. Flip the eggs and fry them on their round sides—jostling them around frequently—until they're heated through, about 3 minutes.

Serve at any temperature. For a simple sandwich, chop Scotch eggs coarsely, top with mayonnaise and mustard, and put it on your favorite bread.

DOUBLE GARLIC DIP

The combination of roasted garlic and fresh garlic means this is a garlic dip to be reckoned with. Guests will mop it up with almost anything in reach: fresh-cut veggies, small pieces of pita or chewy country bread, crackers, tortilla chips, and so forth. It also works well as a salad dressing. One fun way to serve it is in an unheated fondue pot. Let your guests skewer the dipping agent of their choice with a fondue fork and dip away. This makes about 1 cup.

In an oiled ramekin, roast 2 cloves of unpeeled garlic in a 350°F oven until the garlic is soft and golden, about 30 minutes. Squeeze the roasted garlic out of its skin. In a food processor, combine the roasted garlic with 1 minced raw clove of garlic, ½ cup plain yogurt, 5 tablespoons mayonnaise, and ¼ teaspoon salt. Process the dip until it is smooth and you don't see big pieces of garlic. Serve immediately or chill for up to 5 days.

GARAM MASALA POPCORN

Garam masala is an Indian spice mixture that you can now find in most supermarkets. It reminds me of Chinese five-spice powder in that it's a combination of both savory and sweet spices, like coriander, cardamom, cinnamon, cloves, and pepper. I have a suspicion it would make an excellent pumpkin pie spice, but I'll save that experiment for another cookbook. For now, enjoy this slightly spicy popcorn. This makes about 8 cups.

To pop the popcorn, put 2 tablespoons canola oil and 3 unpopped kernels in a 3- to 4-quart stock pot, cover, and heat over medium-high heat until the first kernel pops, then add ⅓ cup kernels to the pot and wait. When the kernels begin popping, shake the pot often to keep the popped kernels from burning. Turn the popcorn out into a bowl and toss it with ¾ teaspoon garam masala (or to taste), ⅛ teaspoon sugar, and ⅛ teaspoon salt. Once it has cooled, the popcorn keeps well in an airtight container at room temperature.

SALADS, SIDES, TWO SOUPS, AND A BREAD

CHIFFONADE SALAD WITH HERBS APLENTY

✴

I think I invented this salad because I love my chef's knife so much. It's just darn fun to chop things, and the ribbons of lettuce and mere threads of mixed herbs make a pretty salad with flavors that mingle and meld more than in most green salads. If you're blessed with your own herb garden, this is the salad to make in the middle of summer when you have more herbs than you know what to do with. The more herbs, the merrier.

Chiffonade is just the French term for something cut into thin ribbons. The easiest way to do this is to roll several lettuce (or herb) leaves together in a snug package and then chop them crosswise—thus making several ribbons at once. Cutting the lettuce and herbs so thin makes them a bit more susceptible to oxidation, so for the best taste, dress this salad immediately and serve it within 30 minutes of making it. (In other words, this isn't the salad to make if you need to drive 4 hours before getting to the picnic site.) Once you have your ingredients ready, it only takes a few minutes to do the chopping and dressing.

SERVES 6

1 bunch romaine lettuce, cut into finger-wide ribbons

2 Belgian endives, cut into ribbons thinner than the romaine

1 cup watercress, cut into ribbons thinner than the romaine

2/3 cup, more or less, mixed fresh herbs such as cilantro, basil, thyme, mint, chives, parsley, cut into very thin ribbons or finely chopped

Olive oil

Freshly squeezed lemon juice

Salt and pepper

Toss the greens and herbs, then drizzle with olive oil, lemon juice, and salt and pepper to taste. For this salad, I prefer to keep the dressing pretty light. Serve the salad as soon as possible, tossing it again briefly just before serving.

CHUNKY SUMMER SALAD WITH PEACHES, TOMATOES, AND FARMER CHEESE

✳

When you want a green salad that has substance but isn't quite a meal in itself, this one's a winner. I love a salad that has big targets for me to stab with my fork. Very satisfying, that. As with all green salads, there's plenty of room for improvisation in this recipe, so try different greens, cheeses, vinegars, etc.

SERVES 6 TO 8

2 large tomatoes

4 medium peaches

1 head red leaf lettuce, washed, dried, and torn into pieces

1 Vidalia onion, cut into very thin half-circles

8 ounces farmer cheese, cut into cubes

¼ cup extra virgin olive oil

2 tablespoons white wine vinegar

2 tablespoons cider vinegar

2 tablespoons freshly squeezed lemon juice

Salt and freshly ground black pepper

To peel the tomatoes and peaches, bring a pot of water to a boil. Boil the tomatoes for 20 seconds, then immediately transfer them to a bowl of ice water. Boil the peaches for 30 seconds and put them in the ice water, too. The skins of the tomatoes and peaches will come off easily. Core the tomatoes and cut them into chunks. Cut the peaches into wedges.

In a salad bowl, layer the salad from bottom to top: lettuce, onion, tomatoes, peaches, and cheese.

To make the vinaigrette, whisk together the olive oil, white wine vinegar, cider vinegar, lemon juice, and salt and pepper to taste. Pour it over the salad.

Serve the salad at room temperature within an hour or so of preparation.

For a picnic, you may want to transport many of the ingredients separately and toss them together just before serving.

SALADE NIÇOISE

✳

Salade Niçoise is a favorite of mine year-round, and it makes an excellent portable meal. Add drinks and maybe some bread and you're good to go. I recommend transporting the salad's components separately and then letting everybody construct their own salad at the picnic. (Now you have a use for all that plastic storage ware.) I also think that the salad should be eaten the same day it's made, preferably as soon as possible. If you've got the ingredients on hand, you can have everything cooked and packed to go in less than 45 minutes.

SERVES 6

1 pound small potatoes, scrubbed and quartered

8 ounces green beans, trimmed

2 heads Bibb, romaine, or leaf lettuce, cleaned, dried,
and torn into pieces

1 pint cherry tomatoes, halved, or ¾ pound larger tomatoes,
in wedges

12 ounces canned tuna in olive oil, drained

1 small red onion, cut into thin half-circles

6 large hard-boiled eggs (see page 114), quartered

30 Niçoise olives

6 to 10 anchovy fillets, optional

2 tablespoons capers, rinsed

VINAIGRETTE

2 shallots, minced

¼ cup white wine vinegar

¼ cup freshly squeezed lemon juice

¾ cup extra virgin olive oil

1/4 cup minced fresh herbs, such as basil, thyme, and oregano
2 teaspoons Dijon mustard
Salt and freshly ground black pepper

Boil the potatoes in salted water until tender, 5 to 10 minutes. Remove the potatoes with a slotted spoon, then boil the green beans in the same water until tender-crisp, 3 to 5 minutes. Remove the beans and immediately rinse them for a minute under cold tap water to stop the cooking.

To make the vinaigrette, whisk together the shallots, white wine vinegar, lemon juice, olive oil, herbs, and mustard. Season to taste with salt and pepper.

Now separately toss the potatoes, beans, lettuce, tomatoes, tuna, and red onion in a little bit of the vinaigrette, and put each ingredient in a transportable container. Be sure to reserve about a quarter of the vinaigrette for later. Also pack the eggs, olives, anchovies, if desired, and capers separately.

At the picnic site, toss the ingredients in their vinaigrette again, then prepare each salad on a large plate in this manner: First create a bed of lettuce. Mound the tuna in the middle. Then separately mound the potatoes, beans, tomatoes, and red onions around the tuna. Put four quarter-sections of the hard-boiled eggs somewhere on each salad and drizzle them with the extra vinaigrette. Lay on the anchovy fillets. And sprinkle on the capers and olives.

Serve immediately.

CELERY AND GREEN APPLE SALAD

✳

This is what I like to call an accent salad, because its pleasant acidity and bright flavor, color, and texture will contrast with—and therefore highlight—whatever it's served with. It's simple to make, beautiful, and refreshing. I'm particularly fond of the slight licorice flavor that floats hauntingly in the background. If you don't have a licorice-flavored liqueur, try a tiny bit of fresh tarragon or some crushed anise or fennel seeds. Or leave it out.

SERVES 8

⅓ cup extra virgin olive oil

3 tablespoons freshly squeezed lemon juice

1 teaspoon Sambuca, anisette, or similar liqueur, or to taste, optional

Salt and freshly ground black pepper

½ bunch celery, washed and trimmed

1 pound (about 3 medium) Granny Smith apples

Whisk together the olive oil, lemon juice, and liqueur. Add salt and pepper to taste.

With the slicing blade of a food processor, slice the celery—including the heart and leaves—very thin. Dice the apples (leaving the skin on). Immediately toss the celery and apples with the vinaigrette, which will prevent the apples from browning. Taste and add more liqueur, salt, and pepper, if desired.

Serve immediately or refrigerate for up to a day. Toss again just before serving.

CORN, CUCUMBER, ET CETERA, SALAD

✳

You could call this chopped salad Midsummer Salad—in honor of the corn, cucumbers, basil, and pepper—but that would belittle the pleasant nutty accents that make this salad unique. You could also call it Confetti Salad, on account of the bright colors, but that would make it sound like something your aunt DeeDee used to make. So really, it should be called Corn, Cucumber, Red Chile Pepper, Lime Juice, White Wine Vinegar, Toasted Sesame Oil, Basil, and Peanut Salad. But that's just too long-winded.

SERVES 6

4 ears sweet corn, shucked and cleaned

1 English hothouse cucumber (about 12 ounces), washed and diced

1 red chile pepper, seeds removed, finely diced

Juice of 1 lime

1 tablespoon white wine vinegar

1 teaspoon toasted sesame oil

8 basil leaves, cut à la chiffonade (see page 56)

Plenty of unsalted, dry-roasted peanuts

Boil the corn until tender, 3 to 5 minutes, then cut the kernels off the cobs. Combine the corn kernels with the cucumber, chile pepper, lime juice, white wine vinegar, and sesame oil and toss to combine. Cover and chill for 1 hour or up to 2 days. Before serving, add the basil and a generous sprinkling of peanuts. Or let guests add their own peanuts.

FENNEL AND WHITE BEAN SALAD

✳

Iʼm pretty sure I didnʼt eat fennel until a few years ago. Shame on me. Itʼs not really my fault, though. Itʼs one of those vegetables that used to be unknown in the small towns of the Midwest, but now I see it in farmerʼs markets and supermarkets alike. Like many, I didnʼt at first understand what it was. It looks like a root vegetable, but itʼs really more akin to celery. Eaten raw—sliced very thin and drizzled with a vinaigrette—its licorice flavor and crunch are wonderful. In this recipe, sautéing the fennel accentuates its natural sweetness.

SERVES 4

1 tablespoon extra virgin olive oil

1 medium fennel bulb, cored and thinly sliced

1 shallot, thinly sliced

1 garlic clove, minced

One 14.5-ounce can white beans, drained

1 tablespoon freshly squeezed lemon juice

2 dashes Tabasco sauce

Salt and freshly ground black pepper to taste

Heat the olive oil over medium heat in a medium skillet. Add the fennel and shallot and sauté, stirring frequently, until the fennel just starts to brown. Add the garlic and continue sautéing until everything is lightly browned—a total of 3 to 5 minutes.

Put the hot fennel into a small serving bowl. Add the remaining ingredients and toss. Serve immediately or within 2 hours.

FAST SQUID SALAD

✳

There's a double meaning in the title. First, squid are very fast swimmers. (When they're alive.) Second, since in this recipe the squid only cooks for fifteen seconds, this dish is one of the fastest around. I can't think of anything else that only cooks for fifteen seconds or less. It might be a record.

You know how when you order calamari in a restaurant it's often rubbery? This means it was cooked too long. Cooking squid quickly is the key to tenderness, as I learned from Russ Parsons's book *How to Read a French Fry*, from which I adapted this recipe.

Fast Squid Salad is yet another of those adaptable recipes. Serve it on, in, or near a nice green salad and you've got a perfect picnic. The recipe makes a lot of lemony–olive oily juice that is the perfect dressing for some baby spinach, for example. You could also serve the squid on bruschetta or as part of a sandwich.

SERVES 4

1 pound cleaned squid, bodies cut into narrow rings, tentacles cut into
3 or 4 pieces (see Note)

¼ cup extra virgin olive oil

¼ cup freshly squeezed lemon juice

1 tablespoon red wine vinegar

1 garlic clove, minced

1 teaspoon salt, or to taste

½ teaspoon crushed red pepper flakes

Just a bit of freshly ground black pepper

Bring several quarts of water to a full boil. Have a colander and a bowl of ice water standing by. Boil the squid for exactly 15 seconds—during which time it will turn white and get slightly stiff—then immediately drain it and put it into the ice water to stop the cooking.

Whisk together the remaining ingredients. Drain the cooked squid and blot it dry, then toss it in the juices. Serve immediately or chill. It's best the day it's made.

Note: *Where I live, it's awfully hard to get fresh squid, but I use frozen squid (fully thawed) very successfully in this recipe. Even if the squid is cleaned when you buy it, rinse and inspect it carefully anyway.*

POTATO SALAD WITH HORSERADISH AND PEAS

✳

Horseradish adds a unique tanginess to this creamy potato salad, but the addition of yogurt tames the horseradish just enough that even people who don't usually like horseradish will fall in love with this recipe. The potato salad is best served chilled the same day it is made, but it can keep a day in the fridge.

SERVES 6

1 pound potatoes, peeled and cut into 1-inch chunks

1/2 cup cooked frozen peas

1/3 cup sliced celery

3 tablespoons prepared horseradish

3 tablespoons mayonnaise

3 tablespoons plain yogurt

Salt and pepper to taste

Boil the potatoes in salted water until tender, 10 to 15 minutes. Drain the potatoes and let them cool a bit before proceeding.

Combine the potatoes with the remaining ingredients and stir. Adjust the salt and pepper as needed. Cover and chill.

ROASTED POTATO SALAD WITH CRÈME FRAÎCHE

✳

I t's simple, but don't let that fool you. By roasting the potatoes until they're brown, you get a lot more flavor than from a boiled or baked potato. The same goes for the garlic. The result is that the comforting roasted flavor carries the whole salad, so there's no need to gunk it up with mayo or mustard. The roasted potatoes are complemented nicely by the tanginess of the vinegar and crème fraîche.

This salad is best within a few hours of being made. Serve at room temperature.

SERVES 6

2 pounds potatoes

3 tablespoons extra virgin olive oil

Salt and freshly ground black pepper

6 garlic cloves, left unpeeled

2 tablespoons sherry vinegar

¾ cup crème fraîche

2 tablespoons toasted pine nuts

Preheat the oven to 450°F. Peel the potatoes and cut them into spears like french fries. Dry each potato spear with a towel. Toss the potatoes thoroughly in a large ovenproof skillet with the olive oil and salt and pepper to taste. Put the potatoes in the oven. Wrap the garlic cloves together in foil and put them next to the potatoes in the oven.

Roast the potatoes for 40 to 50 minutes, stirring and turning them about every 15 minutes. When they have formed dark crusts, they're done. Remove the garlic at the same time.

Cut the potatoes while still hot into small chunks (a serrated knife works well). Toss the hot potatoes in a bowl with the vinegar. Press the soft garlic pulp out of the garlic cloves and mash it to a paste with a fork. Add the garlic to the potatoes and toss again.

When the potatoes have cooled slightly, spread the crème fraîche on top, then sprinkle on the pine nuts.

CHICKEN SALAD WITH GRAPES, TARRAGON, AND TOASTED WALNUTS

✳

This is the kind of chicken salad to write home about: *Dear Mom, I met a fantastic chicken salad. I never thought I'd feel this way about a chicken salad, but I do. The sweetness of the grapes plays off the richness of the walnuts, and the gentle licorice flavor of the tarragon pulls the whole thing together. It's everything I've ever dreamed about in a chicken salad. It's all I've ever wanted. . . .*

SERVES 6

2/3 cup chopped walnuts

4 skinless, boneless chicken breast halves, cooked and cut into small pieces

1 cup chopped celery

1 cup seedless grape halves

6 tablespoons mayonnaise

2 tablespoons chopped fresh tarragon

2 teaspoons lemon juice, or to taste

Salt and pepper to taste

Toast the walnuts in a skillet over medium-high heat, stirring frequently, until they are fragrant and starting to darken, about 5 minutes.

Combine the walnuts with the remaining ingredients and stir. Chill the salad for at least an hour, or up to 24 hours. Serve on greens, fresh tomato slices, or bread.

SUBSTANTIAL CORNBREAD SALAD

✳

Salads made with old or stale bread exist worldwide. In the United States, southerners make a cornbread salad with tomatoes, green pepper, onion, sweet pickles, bacon, and a whole cup of mayonnaise (or, more likely, Miracle Whip). It's a great potluck dish and I included a recipe for it in my first cookbook, but I figured it was time for a cornbread salad makeover. My basic guiding principle was just to put in everything I loved. It worked.

SERVES 8 TO 10

1 pound leftover cornbread (about ¾ of an 8 × 8-inch pan)
(See Note)

1 pint cherry tomatoes, halved, or 2 small to medium tomatoes, chopped

1 medium red onion, diced

⅔ cup chopped fresh cilantro

¼ cup olive oil

2 tablespoons rice vinegar

1 ripe avocado, cut into cubes

6 slices cooked bacon, chopped into small bits

⅓ cup mayonnaise

Cut the cornbread into 1-inch cubes, then toast it on a baking sheet in a 350°F oven until it's somewhat dry, turning once, about 10 minutes.

Toss the tomatoes, red onion, cilantro, olive oil, and rice vinegar together. Separately stir together the avocado cubes, bacon, and mayonnaise.

In a serving bowl, layer half the cornbread on the bottom. Top it with half the tomato mixture, then add dabs of half the avocado mixture. Repeat the layers. Serve immediately or chill for up to a day.

Note: *Any cornbread will work well, but for this salad I prefer a softer, cakier cornbread with some sugar.*

NOODLES WITH WALNUT AND BLUE CHEESE PESTO

✳

This quick pasta dish makes for a great light picnic. Serve it with a bottle of Riesling and some juicy, ripe pears—which go so well with both walnuts and blue cheese. A green salad would be a welcome addition, too. For an impromptu picnic, you can prepare this dish and be out the door in half an hour.

SERVES 4

12 ounces spaghetti or other noodle

1 cup walnuts

1 cup (about 4 ounces) crumbled blue cheese

½ cup loosely packed fresh flatleaf parsley, plus more for garnish

1 garlic clove

½ teaspoon paprika

Salt and freshly ground pepper

¼ cup extra virgin olive oil, or as needed

Bring a big pot of water to a boil. Salt the water and boil the pasta until it is tender, then drain.

In a food processor, combine the walnuts, blue cheese, parsley, garlic, paprika, and a bit of salt and pepper. Process briefly, until there are no big chunks of anything remaining.

With the processor running, drizzle the oil into the mixture, adding just enough to make a thick and smooth pesto about the consistency of hummus. Taste for salt and pepper.

Toss the warm noodles with the pesto until the noodles are coated.

For a picnic, serve the noodles at room temperature or cold. The noodles can be refrigerated for a day. For dining at home, or a backyard picnic, the noodles are also good warm.

COUSCOUS WITH GREEN BEANS AND HAZELNUTS

✳

One of the reasons you should be cooking with couscous more often is that it cooks *fast*. It's the sprinter of the grain/pasta world. It's done in a fraction of the time it takes to cook rice, for instance. Of course, other reasons to enjoy couscous are its versatility and gentle nutty flavor. Last, but not least, is the name itself. Couscous.

Green beans, hazelnuts, and couscous are a perfect little trio. I could eat a whole big bowl of it myself. In fact, I have.

MAKES 6 TO 8 SERVINGS

⅔ cup raw hazelnuts

1 cup couscous

8 ounces fresh green beans, washed and trimmed

6 tablespoons extra virgin olive oil

2 tablespoons red wine vinegar

Salt and freshly ground black pepper

2 scallions, cut into thin rounds (white and light green parts only)

Preheat the oven to 350°F. Toast the hazelnuts, spreading on a baking sheet and baking until they are slightly darker and fragrant, about 10 minutes. Let them cool a bit and then rub off their skins with your hands, if desired. Don't worry about removing all the skins. Put them in a plastic bag and pound them with a rolling pin or mallet to break them into smallish pieces—this is easier than chopping them with a knife.

To cook the couscous, bring 1½ cups water to a boil. Stir in the couscous, let it come to a boil, then lower the heat, cover the pan, and let it simmer just until all the water is absorbed, 2 to 4 minutes. Stir the couscous, then let it stand, covered, while you cook the beans.

For the green beans, bring plenty of salted water to a boil. Drop the beans in and boil them just until they're getting tender-crisp, about 3 minutes. Transfer them immediately to a bowl of ice water. Once they've cooled, cut them into bite-size pieces.

Whisk together the olive oil, vinegar, and salt and pepper to taste.

In a serving bowl, toss the nuts, couscous, green beans, and scallions. Stir in the vinaigrette.

For a picnic, serve the dish at room temperature or cold. The dish can be refrigerated for 2 days. For dining at home, or a backyard picnic, the dish is also good served warm.

CHICKPEAS IN INTRIGUING TOMATO SAUCE

✳

This easy tomato sauce packs just a hint of heat and spiciness, transforming plain-Jane chickpeas into a unique and versatile side dish. The sauce can do the same for cold rice or lentils.

SERVES 6

2 tablespoons extra virgin olive oil

½ medium onion, finely chopped

3 garlic cloves, minced

One 14-ounce can diced tomatoes, with their juice

½ teaspoon ground caraway seeds

¼ teaspoon crushed red pepper flakes

Plenty of freshly ground black pepper

Two 15-ounce cans chickpeas, drained and rinsed

Heat the oil over medium heat in a medium skillet. Sauté the onion until it begins to soften, about 3 minutes. Add the garlic and continue cooking until the onion starts to turn golden brown, about another 5 minutes.

Stir in the tomatoes and their juice, caraway seeds, red pepper flakes, and black pepper. Simmer, stirring occasionally, until the mixture thickens, about 10 minutes. Puree the sauce in a blender or food processor, then return it to the skillet and stir in the chickpeas. Add salt, if needed.

For a picnic, serve at room temperature or cold. The chickpeas can be refrigerated for 2 days. For dining at home or a backyard picnic, the dish is also good warm.

QUICK PICKLED BEETS

✳

Pickled beets were a favorite of my family when I was growing up, and we canned several pints of our garden beets every year. Pickled beets still show up on "relish trays" across the Midwest, and are extremely easy to make. This recipe is the exact recipe my mother still uses to can beets, except it's scaled down to make one pint. We eat them as a cold vegetable side dish with almost anything in any season. If you can find tiny baby beets, pickle them whole for a darling appetizer.

MAKES ABOUT 6 SERVINGS

1 pound washed and trimmed beets

7 tablespoons sugar

6 tablespoons apple cider vinegar

½ teaspoon salt

Boil the beets until tender—15 to 45 minutes, depending on size—then drop them into cold water and peel them. If the beets are small, slice them into ¼-inch rounds; quarter larger beets before slicing. Set the beets aside in a heat-resistant bowl or jar.

Make a pickling syrup by combining the sugar, vinegar, salt, and 1½ tablespoons water in a small saucepan. Bring the syrup to a boil—stirring a couple of times to help the sugar dissolve—then pour the syrup over the beets.

Let the beets cool down before covering and refrigerating them. The beets keep for several weeks in the refrigerator. Serve them cold or at room temperature, with or without their pickling juice.

When transporting them for a picnic, take care to ensure that the juice doesn't leak and stain everything in sight.

SEARED BRUSSELS SPROUTS

✳

We tend to think of brussels sprouts as autumnal vegetables, but if you frequent farmer's markets (or grow them yourself), you know that they first appear in July—smack in the middle of summer. Sometimes you can find whole stalks of them at the market; they look like little cabbages on a tree trunk. This recipe comes from my girl-friend, Kelly. By boiling the sprouts, she rids them of their famous skunky flavor. But the real magic comes in the frying pan, where the sprouts caramelize beautifully. Best of all, they're good served at any temperature, which makes them ideal picnic fare.

SERVES 6

1 pound (about 3 cups) brussels sprouts

3 tablespoons extra virgin olive oil

2 garlic cloves, minced

Salt

Bring a big pot of water to a boil. Boil the brussels sprouts until they're bright green and tender, about 5 to 10 minutes. Drain the sprouts and rinse under cold water to stop the cooking.

Trim the stem of each sprout and peel off any wilted or unhealthy leaves. Cut each sprout in half.

In a skillet large enough to hold the sprouts in a single layer, heat the oil over medium heat. Add the garlic, stir for a few moments, then add salt to taste and the sprouts. Shake or stir the sprouts periodically to keep them from sticking. If necessary, add more oil.

As the sprouts cook, they will smell skunky. Then they will start to brown (caramelize). Finally, they will emit a nutty smell, when they're close to charring. Then they're done. Don't be timid about browning the sprouts—it's almost impossible to overcook them.

For a picnic, serve the sprouts at room temperature or cold. They can be refrigerated for 2 days. For dining at home, or a backyard picnic, the sprouts are terrific served hot.

ASPARAGUS WITH HARD-BOILED EGGS

✳

When the first asparagus of the season hits the farmer's market, this side-dish-slash-salad is the perfect showcase. When a dish is elegant without being fussy, I'm won over instantly. My girlfriend said she would be impressed with anyone who brought this to a picnic. For the record: me too.

Because of the eggs, this dish could work as a main course for a light vegetarian picnic, served with bread, cheese, fruit, and white wine.

SERVES 4 TO 6

2 shallots, thinly sliced

1½ tablespoons red wine vinegar, plus more for pickling

1 pound fresh asparagus, trimmed

4 hard-boiled eggs (see page 114)

3 tablespoons extra virgin olive oil

Salt and freshly ground pepper

Put the sliced shallots in a small cup and cover them with red wine vinegar. Set aside.

Arrange the asparagus in a large skillet with the tips all facing the same direction. Add enough cold water to almost cover. Bring to a boil, then reduce the temperature and simmer for 2 to 5 minutes, just until the asparagus is slightly tender. Immediately drain the asparagus and rinse under cold water to stop the cooking. Arrange the asparagus in a small gratin dish or casserole.

Drain the shallots and rinse them briefly under cold water, then sprinkle them on the asparagus. Cut the eggs into quarters and arrange them on the asparagus.

Whisk together the olive oil, the 1½ tablespoons vinegar, and salt and pepper to taste, then pour the vinaigrette over the asparagus and eggs. Sprinkle with more salt and pepper, if desired.

For a picnic, serve the dish cold or at room temperature. It can be refrigerated for up to 2 days, though if you plan to chill it for long, toss it just before serving and add the eggs at the last minute. For dining at home, or a backyard picnic, the dish is great served warm.

CRISP GREEN BEANS IN JALAPEÑO OIL

✳

Because they're only cooked until they're barely tender, these beans are bright green. And because they're coated with a thin layer of oil, they glisten and shine. It all makes for a darn pretty bowl of beans, if I do say so myself. But the flavor's the thing: simultaneously warm and cool, rich and austere, raw and cooked. It's one of those dishes that adds up to more than the sum of its parts. Got some cold mashed potatoes? Drizzle the oil over them for a real treat. Or put the beans on them *and* drizzle the oil on them. There are no rules. . . .

SERVES 6 TO 8

1 pound green beans, trimmed

1 jalapeño pepper, stemmed and finely chopped

¼ cup canola or vegetable oil

2 shallots, finely chopped

1 teaspoon salt

½ teaspoon sugar

Freshly ground black pepper to taste

Bring a pot of salted water to a boil and drop the beans in. Boil them for 2 to 5 minutes, just until they're tender. Immediately drain the beans in a colander and cool them off by running cold water over them for a minute, tossing them to make sure all the beans cool down. Set the colander aside, allowing the beans to dry as you proceed.

If you want a mild oil, remove all the jalapeño's veins and seeds. For a modest amount of heat, remove some or none of the veins and seeds.

Heat the oil in a heavy skillet over medium heat. Add the jalapeño and shallots and sauté just until the shallots are light brown, about 5 minutes. Remove the skillet from the heat and let the oil sit for 10 minutes. The shallots will brown a bit more from the residual heat.

Whisk in the remaining ingredients, then toss the beans and oil together. Chill the beans until you're ready to serve them. Toss again immediately before serving.

CHILLED AVOCADO AND CUCUMBER SOUP

✳

Cool, tangy, and smooth, this summery fern green soup is an ideal first course: it enlivens your palate without filling you up. But keep the portions small. Or for a light picnic serve it alone with pita bread. I also like it with tortilla chips because its flavors remind me of guacamole. An ideal main course to follow this soup would be Roasted Poblano Quiche with Queso Fresco (page 131). For extra color, garnish the soup with edible flower petals, such as nasturtium or marigold.

SERVES 6

1 ripe avocado

1 cup peeled, seeded, chunked cucumber (about ⅔ medium cucumber), plus more for garnish

1 scallion, coarsely chopped

1 garlic clove

¼ cup packed fresh cilantro, plus more for garnish

2 tablespoons freshly squeezed lemon juice, or to taste

½ cup plain yogurt

4 dashes Tabasco sauce

⅛ teaspoon ground cumin

Salt and freshly ground black pepper to taste

Edible flower pedals for garnish, optional

Cut the avocado in half, discard the seed, and scoop out the flesh. Combine all the ingredients in a blender. Add ½ cup water and ½ cup ice cubes. Blend the soup until it is smooth. Taste and add salt and lemon juice if needed. Garnish the soup with finely chopped cucumber, cilantro, and edible flower petals, if desired.

For a picnic, the soup can be chilled for up to 2 days and served cold. Transport the soup in a thermos or covered pitcher so that it's easy to pour into individual bowls. For dining at home, or a backyard picnic, you can also serve the soup immediately.

ROASTED RED BELL PEPPER SOUP

✴

Here's the kind of soup good in any season and at any serving temperature. Roasting the red peppers brings out their sweetness, but balances it with that wonderful slightly smoky charred flavor. Garnish the soup with chopped parsley and feta cheese, or croutons. Or for a note of acidity, drizzle it sparingly with balsamic vinegar. You may notice I don't use canned chicken broth here. I think it's expensive and doesn't add that much to a carefully crafted soup. Homemade chicken stock, on the other hand, is another story, but a bit time-consuming for our purposes here.

SERVES 4

4 red bell peppers

1 onion, diced

2 garlic cloves, minced

2 tablespoons olive oil

½ teaspoon ground nutmeg

¼ teaspoon ground white pepper

1 bay leaf

Pinch of cayenne pepper

2 tablespoons heavy cream

Salt

Wash the peppers and arrange them on a sturdy baking sheet. Roast them about 4 inches beneath the broiler element, turning them as needed so that all sides of the peppers are blackened. Place the hot peppers in an airtight plastic storage bag so that the steam loosens their skins. After 15 minutes, peel the peppers, remove their cores and seeds, and chop them coarsely.

In a soup pot over medium heat, add the olive oil and sauté the onion, garlic, nutmeg, pepper, bay leaf, and cayenne, stirring frequently, until the garlic is well browned but not burned, about 10 minutes. Add the peppers and 2 cups water, bring to a boil, then simmer, partially covered, for 15 minutes.

Remove the bay leaf, stir in the cream, and puree the soup—either in batches in a blender or with an immersion blender right in the pot. Add salt to taste.

Since the soup is good at any temperature, transport it in a thermos if you want to keep it hot or cold. This also makes it easy to pour into individual bowls. The soup can be chilled for up to 3 days (and reheated, if desired).

OVERNIGHT CIABATTA
(BREAD OF THE AGES)

✳

Sure, this recipe takes time—and who really wants to fire up their oven for a couple of hours during prime picnic season?—but what picnic book would be complete without a recipe for the kind of bread you can make a picnic out of with just a bit of cheese and some wine? This is that bread. Ciabatta is an Italian loaf that is low-slung, chewy, and full of wonderful holes inside.

I developed this recipe using the formula and technique for *pain à l'ancienne* from Peter Reinhart's masterwork, *The Bread Baker's Apprentice*. Many home bakers know that slowing down the "rising" or fermentation of the dough improves the flavor of many yeast breads. This recipe achieves that by refrigerating the dough overnight. It's that simple—no starter, no wild yeast, not even any punching down. The ciabatta is nutty, chewy, faintly sweet, and beautiful. You don't even have to pack a bread knife: just tear off chunks of this rustic bread. I think a fitting name for this bread—echoing *pain à l'ancienne*—is Bread of the Ages.

The bread is best the day it's made, of course, but it will only go slightly stale if you store it for a day in a paper bag. You can freeze it, too, but because it's such a lean bread it will dry out a bit when you reheat it.

MAKES 3 MEDIUM LOAVES

3½ cups (15.625 ounces) King Arthur unbleached all-purpose flour,
or unbleached bread flour

1¼ teaspoons salt

1 teaspoon instant yeast (see Note)

1⅜ to 1¾ cups ice-cold water

Olive oil, for greasing

In the bowl of a standing mixer, mix the flour, salt, yeast, and 1⅜ cups ice water on low speed with the paddle for 2 minutes. Then attach the dough hook and mix on medium speed for 5 minutes. During this mixing, the dough should come together and pull away from the sides of the bowl, but not the bottom. If it doesn't come away from the sides of the bowl, sprinkle in a bit more flour as needed. And if it isn't sticking to the bottom of the bowl, dribble in more ice-cold water as needed.

Lightly grease a medium bowl with olive oil. Transfer the dough to the bowl, spread a small amount of olive oil over the top of the dough, cover the bowl tightly with plastic wrap, and refrigerate overnight.

The next day, 4 to 6 hours before baking the bread, remove the dough from the refrigerator (notice that it has risen slightly) and let it sit in the bowl *at room temperature* until it has nearly doubled in size, 2 to 4 hours.

Sprinkle your counter generously with flour (this is a very sticky dough), then turn the dough out gently onto the flour. Sprinkle flour generously on top of the dough. Handling the dough gently, stretch it into a rough rectangle about the size of a piece of paper. With a wet bench knife, cut the dough into 3 long pieces. Each piece will be about a foot long and a few inches wide. Don't worry about perfect shapes: this is a rustic bread with lots of character.

Cut 3 pieces of parchment paper a bit larger than each piece of dough and gently transfer each piece of dough onto the parchment. Cover the loaves with plastic wrap and let them sit at room temperature for about 2 hours, until they're very puffy.

Forty-five minutes before baking, put a baking stone on the bottom rack of the oven. Set a cast-iron skillet alongside it or on a higher rack. Preheat the oven to 450°F.

When the loaves are ready, transfer them to a pizza peel, then slide them onto the hot stone, parchment and all—being sure no parchment hangs over the edge of the stone. (If you can't fit all 3 loaves on the stone at once, bake them in shifts, giving the oven 15 minutes to reheat between shifts.) Immediately pour 1 cup water into the hot cast-iron skillet and close the oven door to trap the steam.

Bake for 15 to 20 minutes, until lightly browned and hollow-sounding when tapped on the bottom. If you use an instant thermometer, the loaves are done when they register 205°F in the center.

Let the ciabatta cool on racks for 20 minutes.

Note: *Active dry yeast should* not *be substituted for the instant yeast.*

"QUICK PIC" SALADS, SOUPS, AND SIDES

✳

CHERRY TOMATO SALAD

I like to make this with those little pear-shaped yellow tomatoes, but all varieties work well, as long as they're ripe. It's a fast salad that looks great and plays well with others. I've been known to make a lunch of it with some good bread. This serves 6.

Slice 20 ounces cherry or grape tomatoes in half. Toss them with a big handful of chopped cilantro (or a lesser amount of basil), a good drizzle of extra virgin olive oil, a smaller amount of balsamic vinegar, and salt and pepper to taste. Finally, add about 1 cup of crumbled goat's cheese (or feta) and toss again briefly. Serve within 2 hours.

COUNTRY COLESLAW

This simple slaw resembles those made by the small-town cooks of my Missouri childhood. It serves 6.

With the slicing blade of a food processor, slice a small head of cabbage and 2 medium carrots. Insert the chopping blade and pulse until the slaw is the desired consistency. Separately whisk together ¼ cup mayonnaise, 3 tablespoons cider vinegar, and 1 tablespoon sugar. Stir this dressing into the slaw, along with ½ to 1 teaspoon celery seeds. Add salt and pepper to taste. Chill for at least 2 hours.

HOPPIN' JOHN

A longtime southern favorite—often served on New Year's Day for good luck—this incarnation of rice and beans was traditionally flavored with less desirable parts of the pig, like hooves and tails. These days, it often has bacon in it, but this vegetarian version, which borrows the cumin and oregano from Caribbean cuisine, is plenty flavorful, and is a winning side dish that can accompany about anything. It serves 6.

Start ½ cup long-grain rice cooking with 1 cup water in a small saucepan. Meanwhile, in another saucepan, sauté one diced onion and one minced garlic clove in 1 tablespoon olive oil. After a bit, add ¼ teaspoon cumin, ¼ teaspoon dried oregano, and salt and pepper. When the onion is very soft, add one 15½-ounce can of black-eyed peas, including the juice. Simmer over medium heat until the liquid thickens, about 15 minutes. Taste for salt. Combine the beans and the cooked rice and serve hot, warm, or at room temperature.

GREEN LENTILS IN VINAIGRETTE

A simple, satisfying side dish for almost any occasion. Put a piece of Laura Calder's Poached Salmon (page 100) on top for a simple picnic entree. This serves 6.

In a saucepan, cover 1 cup French du Puy lentils with 2 inches water. Bring to a boil, then lower the heat and simmer until tender, 30 to 40 minutes. Drain the lentils, then toss with half a recipe of the vinaigrette from the Salade Niçoise (page 60). Toss again immediately before serving. Serve at any temperature.

A FRENCH INTERLUDE

A Letter from Laura Calder
with a Picnic Menu

Around the time my first cookbook came out, my editor sent me another first book by one of her writers. It was *French Food at Home*, and the author was Laura Calder, who is about my age. Now, I'm not sure how other people do these things, but when I get my hands on a promising new cookbook, I spend a lot of time flipping through it, reading here and there, imagining the dishes being described, picturing the author's kitchen, and basically picking out recipes to try. When I find a recipe I want to cook, I mark the page with a Post-it note. As I continue to read and use a cookbook, I add more notes. Thus, it is easy to pull a cookbook from my shelf and tell how well loved it is simply by how many notes are sticking out of it. By this measure, Laura's book set a record, I think. The recipes were delightful and unburdened, and the writing was as good as that of any novel. (My girlfriend and I still talk about Laura's headnote for Brandade Peppers: "So you have to soak the cod and that scares you.")

In other words, I loved the book, and it turned out that Laura liked my book, too, so we struck up a correspondence. We food writers have to stick together, after all. When she volunteered to give me a few French recipes for my picnic book, I knew they would be a perfect fit, and a good way to pay homage to the great food of France.

Someday, when Laura and I actually meet each other, I'll make cornbread and she'll make something French that will put me to shame. I'm looking forward to it.

July 2004
Château du Feij
Burgundy, France

Dear Jeremy,

The truth about most French picnics is that nobody cooks a
thing. Everyone just goes to the cheese shop for cheeses, to the
baker for bread, to the charcuterie for *saucissons,* to the wine
shop for wine, to the greengrocer for fruit. Then they slip a knife
and a corkscrew into their pocket and head for the park.

There are other ways to approach French picnics, though. Since
I'm living at the moment high on a hillside in remote Burgundy,
six kilometers to the nearest proper town, if I did a picnic
tomorrow I'd be inspired to get much more sumptuous about it
all. I love the idea of juxtaposing the great outdoors with
extreme civilization, so my French picnic would go like this:

I'd drag an iron table out across the lawn and set it up under the
chestnut trees, then I'd drape a great cloth over it (preferably
one with wigged eighteenth-century men in knee-breeches
printed on it, flirting with corseted, but corruptible, ladies). I
would banish plastic and paper from the site and cart out china
and sterling and carafes for wine. I'd need good, solid chairs with
pillows on them. A stack of shawls (in case a wind came up).
Crystal glasses. And all the time in the world to eat!

I'd start the picnic at two in the afternoon, I think. I'd wear a
dress: some flimsy thing that would be comfortable to sprawl on

the lawn in under the sun for a nap after eating. At some stage, there would be a racy game of limbo.

So that's the scene. Now, the food. I'd put platters of everything on the table all at once and let people help themselves slowly, wantonly, whenever they liked while we all got unabashedly drunk on chilled rosé. Even though we'd approach the food in a graze-y way, it wouldn't be graze-y food—not a zillion little bits and bites of this and that, in other words. Instead, I'd just make a regular meal, every dish of which could be served at room temperature.

I'd buy olives and artisanal sausage to keep our heads from spinning during the apéritif. Then I'd serve poached salmon with cherry tomato and basil vinaigrette; baby potatoes with olive oil and fleur de sel; haricots verts with shallots and toasted pine nuts. There would be country bread from the best baker around and very good cheeses (a Basque sheep cheese, a blue from the Auvergne, and a bulging Brie). We'd need a great green salad flecked with herbs and scattered with bright nasturtiums. For the finale—ta-dah!—my plum tart painted purple. It's all easy to make; simple, light, and delicious; unpretentious; and just original enough, without being attention seeking.

So that's my French picnic. Will you come?

Laura

GREAT GREEN SALAD

✳

Laura writes:

Now, my salad. It's basically mixed greens (some soft, you know, some crisp, some flat, some curly, some red, some green, etc.). Then, lots and lots of herbs, not chopped, necessarily, but with the stems off. So, flat parsley leaves, chopped thyme, tarragon leaves, chervil leaves, and chopped chives—whatever's around, really. And, nasturtium blossoms if there are any in the garden. And MY dressing, which goes like this:

A spoonful of Dijon mustard whisked up with salt and pepper and a few squirts of soy sauce (imperatively from the health food store because the cheap stuff is wretched and sharp, not rich, which is the point of it), and a few spoonfuls of balsamic vinegar (although, I'm wondering about raspberry as I write this . . .). So then you whisk in lots and lots of walnut oil and olive oil (amounts depend on how strong each oil is and what will make the right balance). Making salad dressing is like tuning a violin, you know, the taste goes up and down, sharp and flat, reeeouuuuuuraaaaaaaawwwwww, until you get just the right note. Salt and pepper. Tossity toss toss. And you have a very complex and beautiful salad, *n'est-ce pas?* Sometimes I put nuts or seeds in there, or even fried bacon, but not with this menu.

POACHED SALMON WITH TOMATO AND BASIL VINAIGRETTE

✳

SERVES 6

1½ pounds salmon fillets, bones removed

Bay leaf

Slice of lemon

⅔ cup olive oil

Several handfuls fresh basil leaves, chopped

2 cups seeded, diced tomatoes or quartered cherry tomatoes

Salt and freshly ground black pepper

Put the fillets in a pan large enough to hold them in a single layer—like a roasting pan or large lidded skillet. Add enough cold water to cover the fish completely. Add the bay leaf and slice of lemon. Bring the water slowly to a boil, cover the pan with a lid, turn off the heat, and let it sit until it's cool enough to touch. Remove the fish, peel off the skin—if there is any—and arrange the fillets on a platter.

For the sauce, stir together the olive oil, basil, and tomatoes. Season with salt and pepper and spoon the sauce over the fish.

HARICOTS VERTS
WITH SHALLOTS AND
TOASTED PINE NUTS

✳

SERVES 6

1 pound green beans

3 tablespoons very finely minced shallots

2 to 3 tablespoons pine nuts, lightly toasted

Olive oil

Salt to taste

Trim the beans, if desired. Also, you can slice them in half, lengthwise, if desired. Cut beans make this pretty dish even prettier.

Cook the beans in lots of boiling salted water, just until they're tender-crisp, 2 to 4 minutes. Drain and rinse under ice-cold water to set the color and stop the cooking. Drain again. Toss the beans with the remaining ingredients.

Serve at room temperature.

BABY POTATOES WITH OLIVE OIL AND FLEUR DE SEL

*

SERVES 6

1½ pounds baby or fingerling potatoes, scrubbed

Olive oil

Fleur de sel

Freshly ground black pepper, optional

Boil the potatoes in plenty of water until they're tender, 10 to 20 minutes. Drain, then toss them with just enough olive oil to coat. Season to taste with the fleur de sel and pepper, if desired.

Serve at room temperature.

PLUM TART PAINTED PURPLE

✳

SERVES UP TO 10

PASTRY

2½ cups all-purpose flour

½ teaspoon salt

2 tablespoons sugar

½ pound (2 sticks) unsalted butter, cut into small cubes

1 teaspoon vanilla extract

TART

2½ pounds black plums, cut into wedges

¼ cup sugar, optional

1 egg white, lightly beaten

For the pastry, mix the flour, salt, and sugar together in a large bowl. Add the butter cubes and pinch them into the flour mixture with your fingers to make fine crumbs. Make a well in the center. Put the vanilla and ⅓ cup very cold water in the well. With your fingers, stir around the well, slowly bringing in more flour, until you have a pastry dough that holds together in a ball, adding more cold water if needed. Cut the ball in two. Pat each half into a brick shape. Wrap and refrigerate for 15 minutes. Meanwhile, preheat the oven to 400°F. Line a sided baking sheet with parchment paper or foil.

Roll out one pastry brick into a 10- by 14-inch rectangle and set it on the baking sheet. Leaving a 1-inch margin all around, lay down a cobblestone alley of plum wedges to cover. Sprinkle over the sugar, if you like things especially sweet.

Roll out the second brick of pastry slightly larger than the first. When you drape it over the plums it should extend at least to the edge of the first pastry. Run your hands over the tart, pushing the pastry gently onto the plums and making a snug rectangular form. Press the pastry edges together lightly. Trim the edges of the pastry, leaving a half-inch margin all around. It will look like a gigantic ravioli. Then, using a fingertip, press the edges of the crusts together to seal. Cut two slits into the top of the tart, large enough to stick a pastry brush into. Brush all over with the beaten egg white. Bake the tart until the top is lightly browned and the juices are bubbly, about 30 minutes.

Remove the tart from the oven. Paint the tart all over with its juices, using a pastry brush: it's possible that the juice will have run out all over the baking sheet, which makes this easy; if not, simply keep dipping the brush into the two vents on the top of the tart. When you're through, the whole tart should be a glossy, reddish purple. Slide the tart onto a cutting board or serving platter. Serve warm or at room temperature.

SANDWICHES AND SUBSTANTIAL COURSES

TUNA CAKES

✳

Easier and cheaper than crab cakes, these are some darn flavorful and versatile little hockey pucks. Put a few of them on top of a green salad for an unbeatable noontime picnic. You can also serve them as appetizers. Or make a sandwich with them: mayonnaise is the perfect partner, but a more inventive sandwich could include feta cheese and greens. They're good at any temperature, and easy to make.

MAKES SIXTEEN 2-INCH CAKES TO SERVE 4 TO 6

2 tablespoons unsalted butter

2 tablespoons all-purpose flour

2/3 cup milk

Two 3-ounce cans water- or olive oil–packed tuna, drained

1 shallot, minced

2 tablespoons grated Parmesan cheese

2 teaspoons lemon juice

2 teaspoons capers, rinsed and drained

Salt and pepper

Cornmeal or fine bread crumbs, for coating

Olive oil, for panfrying

In a medium skillet, melt the butter over medium heat. Stir in the flour and let the mixture bubble for a minute. Off the heat, slowly stir in the milk. Return the mixture to the heat and let it cook for a few minutes, stirring to deter lumps.

Transfer the white sauce to a bowl and stir in the tuna, shallot, Parmesan, lemon juice, capers, and salt and pepper to taste. Chill the mixture for at least 2 hours, or overnight. This makes it much easier to form patties.

Shape the mixture into little 2-inch-round cakes. Coat the cakes with the cornmeal or bread crumbs. Heat a very thin layer of olive oil in a non-stick skillet over medium heat, then fry the cakes until quite brown—about 3 minutes per side. Let the cakes drain on paper towels.

For a picnic, serve the tuna cakes at room temperature or cold. They can be refrigerated for 2 days. For dining at home, or a backyard picnic, the tuna cakes are also extremely good served warm.

HAM BISCUITS

✳

You're likely to find ham biscuits, something of a southern favorite, on brunch tables, but I find that they make a nearly ideal
picnic sandwich—flavorful, packable, and quite a treat. Wrap them individually in foil after broiling, swaddle them in tea towels in the bottom
of your picnic basket, and they'll keep warm for up to an hour. Count on
serving two biscuits per person. An ingenious way to use leftover biscuits.

MAKES 8 BISCUITS

1 recipe Buttermilk Biscuits (page 110)
Thinly sliced country or city ham
Thinly sliced Swiss cheese
3 tablespoons unsalted butter, softened
3 tablespoons Dijon mustard
3 tablespoons Worcestershire sauce

Preheat the broiler with a rack placed about 8 inches away from the
broiler element.

Split the biscuits. Layer a small amount of ham on the bottom halves of
the biscuits. Top with a slice or two of cheese.

Mix the butter, mustard, and Worcestershire sauce until combined, then
spread the mixture on the top halves of the biscuits.

Broil both halves of the biscuits open-faced on a baking sheet, until
the cheese is bubbly. Assemble the biscuits—putting the halves back
together—and either serve immediately or wrap individually in foil.

HORSERADISH HAM BISCUITS

✳ Follow the above recipe, but omit the Worcestershire sauce
and add a tablespoon or so of prepared horseradish. You can
omit the mustard, too, if desired.

TOMATO AND THYME HAM BISCUITS

✳ Spread cream cheese on the bottom half of the biscuit,
sprinkle it with freshly ground black pepper, then add the ham.
On the top, put a slice of tomato, a smattering of fresh thyme
leaves, and a drizzle of olive oil.

BUTTERMILK BISCUITS

✳

These are do-anything, go-anywhere biscuits. They're tender and flavorful enough to star in a simple breakfast with applesauce, but they're just as good on a picnic the next day as the bread for little sandwiches like Ham Biscuits (page 108), crumbled as part of Biscuits, Berries, Honey, and Cream (page 156), or used for Cinnamon-Buttered Split Biscuits (page 203). Because they're filling biscuits, I present a one-baking-sheet-size recipe here, but feel free to double it. Don't be afraid of a little lard: it makes a terrific biscuit, has less fat than butter, and has none of the dastardly trans fats of vegetable shortening.

These biscuits also make for a fine berry shortcake rendition.

MAKES 8 SQUARE BISCUITS

1½ cups all-purpose flour

2 teaspoons baking powder

½ teaspoon baking soda

½ teaspoon salt

3 tablespoons lard or vegetable shortening, chilled

2 tablespoons unsalted butter, chilled

¾ cup plus 2 tablespoons buttermilk or sour cream

Preheat the oven to 450°F. Have a baking sheet ready.

Sift the flour, baking powder, baking soda, and salt together in a large bowl. With a pastry cutter, cut in the lard and butter until the largest bits are pea-size. Make a well in the center of the mixture and pour in the buttermilk. Stir in the buttermilk just until the dough comes together. Don't overmix—the next step will incorporate any remaining bits of dry flour.

Turn the dough out onto a floured counter. With floured hands (and bench knife, if you have one) pat the dough gently flat and then fold it over onto itself and pat it gently again. Repeat this a total of four times, then pat the dough into a square or rectangle ½ inch thick and cut square biscuits with a sharp pizza cutter, trimming off the rough edges. The square shape makes a nice sandwich biscuit and minimizes the left-over scraps.

Bake the biscuits on the baking sheet, along with any extra scraps, for 10 to 14 minutes, until puffed and browned.

UPSIDE-DOWN MEATLOAF

✳

What's better and more satisfying than a meatloaf sandwich? Beats me. I like 'em simple: sandwich bread (preferably toasted), mayo, thin slices of meatloaf, crisp lettuce, and maybe a couple of dill pickle slices. Ohhhhhhhh, they're divine. And packable! For sandwiches, I wanted a meatloaf recipe that would never come out dry on top or fat-soaked on the bottom, so I devised this simple upside-down baking method to keep the loaf moist and tender but let just the right amount of fat drain away. Well, I admit it ain't no looker, but since when has meatloaf been beautiful? Serve it on a Thursday or Friday for a hot meal, then make sandwiches with the leftovers for a weekend picnic.

**SERVES 4 TO 6 AS A MAIN COURSE, OR
MAKES ABOUT 8 SANDWICHES**

1 pound ground chuck

½ pound ground pork

1 cup fine fresh bread crumbs (from about 2 slices of bread)

¼ cup milk

1 large egg, beaten

3 shallots, finely chopped

1 jalapeño pepper, seeded, cored, and finely chopped

2 tablespoons ketchup

1½ teaspoons salt

Freshly ground black pepper

Preheat the oven to 350°F. With your hands, mix all the ingredients until uniform and put the mixture into an 8½ × 4½ × 3-inch loaf pan.

Set a rack over a baking sheet, then set a sheet of aluminum foil just bigger than the loaf pan on the rack. Make a couple of slits in the middle of the foil. Invert the loaf pan onto the foil. As the loaf bakes, it will drop onto the foil. Because the loaf is never directly in contact with the hot air of the oven, it will remain moist. Some of the excess liquid will leak onto the baking sheet.

Bake for 1 hour and 15 minutes. If making sandwiches, chill before slicing.

EGG SALAD IDEAS

✳

I've long been a big fan of egg salad, even though it's been out of vogue for decades. On the other hand, has it ever been *in* vogue? Maybe not, and maybe that's one of the reasons it's so great: it's a modest creature, but it tastes good every time.

HARD-BOILED EGGS

Everyone seems to have their own method for hard-boiling eggs, and here's mine, which works every time and rarely cracks an egg.

In a saucepan, cover the eggs with enough cold water to cover them by at least an inch. Bring the water to a boil, then immediately remove the pan from the heat and cover it. Let the eggs sit for 18 minutes, then drain them and cool them off by either putting them in an ice bath or leaving them in the pan and running cold water onto them for several minutes. This cooldown helps prevent that harmless but unattractive green aura around the yolks.

When the eggs are cool, you can peel them. It's easiest to roll the egg around first, making a network of cracks over the entire shell. Start with the blunt end of the egg and peel them under running water. Older eggs peel more easily than fresh eggs.

If you don't plan to use the eggs soon, you can refrigerate unpeeled hard-boiled eggs for a week. A trick to tell hard-boiled eggs from raw eggs is to spin them like a top. Hard-boiled eggs spin easily. Raw eggs fall over.

CLASSIC EGG SALAD

MAKES 3 SANDWICHES

4 hard-boiled eggs

2 to 3 tablespoons mayonnaise, or to taste

1 to 2 tablespoons prepared mustard, if desired

Salt and pepper to taste

Put all the ingredients in a small bowl and chop until you reach the desired consistency. I use a knife and fork—the knife cuts, the fork blends.

For a large batch of egg salad, you can chop the eggs in a food processor—very briefly—before stirring in the other ingredients.

EGG SALAD ADDITIONS AND PARTNERS

thinly sliced fennel

baby arugula

tomato slices

sprouts

capers

finely chopped chives

sunflower greens

chopped sweet pickles

cucumber rounds

crisp romaine lettuce leaves

raisins (my favorite!)

serve on toasted English muffins

serve in pita bread

CORNISH BEEF PASTIES

✴

The hearty handheld meal known as the pasty—rhymes with nasty—originated long ago in the mining districts of Cornwall. The miners' hands were so filthy they held these portable pies by the thick rim of crust that rings them, then discarded the dirty crust. Pasties came to the United States when Cornish miners started working the copper and iron mines in the Upper Peninsula of Michigan. Designed for easy transportation—and good at any temperature—these are good picnic fare for cooler weather, especially for hikers and fishermen who have worked up sizable appetites. Half a pasty will suit modest appetites.

MAKES 4 PASTIES TO SERVE 4 TO 8

Double recipe Whole Wheat Quiche Pastry, chilled (page 133)

12 ounces sirloin steak or round steak, cut into ¼-inch cubes

¾ cup diced potatoes

1 medium turnip, diced

1 medium carrot, diced

1 small onion, diced

1 tablespoon chopped fresh flatleaf parsley, optional

1½ teaspoons salt

Freshly ground black pepper

Preheat the oven to 400°F. Divide the chilled quiche pastry into 4 pieces and roll each into a circle a bit larger than a dinner plate.

Combine all the filling ingredients. Place a quarter of the filling on half of each crust, then fold the other half over and crimp the edge shut by making a series of small folds. Cut three slits in the top of each pasty.

Bake the pasties on an ungreased baking sheet for 50 minutes. Let rest for 10 minutes before serving. If you're not planning to eat them within an hour, refrigerate them.

BARBECUE SHREDDED PORK

✳

Who knew making your own "pulled" pork sandwiches could be so easy? I sure didn't. Okay, barbecue diehards will tell you that you're supposed to cook the pork for several hours over smoldering hardwood charcoal. And the twenty-minute barbecue sauce might give Texas- or Carolina-style sauce purists conniptions. But who cares whether it's authentic or not as long as it's wholesome and plate-licking good? Not me. Serve the pork on good hamburger buns with Country Coleslaw (page 92), potato chips, dill pickles, and iced tea, and you've got an American picnic to beat all.

SERVES 4 TO 6

1½ pounds pork shoulder steaks

½ cup white vinegar

½ cup cider vinegar

¼ cup plus 2 tablespoons light or dark brown sugar

8 tablespoons (1 stick) unsalted butter

2 garlic cloves, minced

2 tablespoons dry mustard

2 teaspoons paprika

2 teaspoons salt

1 teaspoon Tabasco sauce

1 teaspoon cayenne pepper

Lots of freshly ground black pepper

Put the pork steaks in a stockpot and cover them with 2 inches water. Bring them to a boil, then reduce the heat and cover. Let the pork simmer for 2½ to 3 hours, adding more water to keep the meat covered, if necessary.

About half an hour before the meat is done, prepare the barbecue sauce. Combine all the remaining ingredients in a medium saucepan and bring them to a full simmer, stirring until the sugar is dissolved. Continue simmering, stirring occasionally, until the sauce thickens nicely, 10 to 20 minutes. Reserve.

Remove the meat and let it cool until you can handle it safely, then shred it by hand, discarding the fat and bones. The meat will be tender and will fall apart in your hands. Don't worry if the pork is a little pink inside—it's done.

Combine the shredded pork with the barbecue sauce. Serve immediately or refrigerate for up to 2 days. For the best results, assemble the sandwiches at the picnic site.

LAMB PITA MEZE

✳

I like a picnic course where everyone can do a little pick-and-choose. The Middle Eastern and North African meze meal is designed around that idea, and it's in the spirit of those meals that I present these spicy lamb pitas with all kinds of toppings. It's a design-your-own sandwich, and it involves no cooking except the lamb filling. Falafels would be a great vegetarian alternative.

Making your sandwich is simple: take half a pita, open it up, spoon in some lamb filling, then top it with as many other parts of the meze as you wish. No two sandwiches are alike!

SERVES 6

LAMB FILLING

4 teaspoons extra virgin olive oil

4 shallots, diced

4 garlic cloves, minced

1 pound lean ground lamb

1⅓ cups diced tomatoes or canned tomatoes, drained and diced

½ cup golden raisins, optional

2 teaspoons freshly squeezed lemon juice

½ teaspoon ground allspice

½ teaspoon ground cinnamon

½ teaspoon cayenne pepper

½ teaspoon ground cumin

Salt and freshly ground black pepper

Heat the olive oil in a large skillet over medium heat and sauté the shallots and garlic until fragrant, 2 to 3 minutes. Add the ground lamb and chop at it with a wooden spoon to break it into small pieces. When the lamb is gray and cooked through, add the tomatoes and cook until nearly all the liquid in the pan is gone. If there's a lot of liquid, you can drain it off.

Stir in all the remaining filling ingredients and remove the mixture from the heat. Taste for salt and pepper.

For a picnic, serve the filling at room temperature or cold. It can be refrigerated for up to 2 days. For dining at home, or a backyard picnic, the filling is also good served warm or hot.

THE SANDWICH _MEZE_
the lamb filling
six or more pitas
Mint and Yogurt Cucumber Relish (page 122)
chopped lettuce or greens
toasted pine nuts
crumbled feta cheese
halved cherry tomatoes
chopped fresh parsley
chopped fresh mint
chopped scallions
chopped red onions soaked for 10 minutes in vinegar and then drained

MINT AND YOGURT CUCUMBER RELISH

✳

The perfect cool and creamy topping for your lamb pita.

---

6 SERVINGS

2 medium cucumbers, peeled and grated

1 cup plain yogurt

1 garlic clove, minced

1 cup loosely packed fresh mint, chopped

½ teaspoon salt

½ teaspoon freshly ground black pepper

Spread the grated cucumber on a baking sheet and sprinkle it with a little salt. Let it sit for 30 minutes, then squeeze the moisture from it with your hands or in cheesecloth or a clean towel. Combine the cucumber with the other ingredients and refrigerate until serving.

SESAME NOODLES

✳

Okay, if you're not yet familiar with the Asian section of your supermarket, this recipe is a darn good reason to explore it. Sure, the ingredients list is a bit long for what's really an extremely simple dish, but once you taste the results, you'll understand how all the parts of the recipe—a tablespoon of this, a quarter cup of that—add layer upon layer of flavor to the lowly noodles. I particularly enjoy how the mild heat of the sauce is balanced by the coolness of the cucumbers.

To make a meal of the dish, add some good old-fashioned protein, like Flavorful Chicken Pieces (page 140) or some simple sautéed shrimp.

SERVES 4 TO 6

8 ounces Asian wheat noodles or thin spaghetti

1 tablespoon raw sesame seeds

¼ cup toasted sesame oil

4 garlic cloves, minced

1 tablespoon minced fresh peeled ginger

3 tablespoons teriyaki sauce

2 tablespoons soy sauce

2 tablespoons lime juice

2 teaspoons chili-garlic sauce

1 small cucumber, peeled, seeded, and cut into half-circles

4 scallions (white and light green parts only), thinly sliced

Salt

Unsalted roasted peanuts, optional

Boil the noodles according to the directions on the package. Drain and rinse under cold water (to prevent them from sticking together).

In a small skillet, toast the sesame seeds over medium-low heat until they just start to brown, 5 to 10 minutes. Reserve the seeds.

In the same skillet, heat the sesame oil over medium heat. When the oil is hot, add the garlic and ginger and sauté for 15 seconds. Then add the teriyaki sauce, soy sauce, lime juice, and chili-garlic sauce. Let come to a simmer and then simmer for 1 minute.

In a bowl, toss the noodles with the sauce. Sprinkle on the toasted sesame seeds. Add salt to taste. Then top with the cucumber, scallions, and peanuts, if desired.

The noodles can be served at room temperature or cold. They can be refrigerated for up to 2 days.

ROTINI WITH FETA AND BABY ARUGULA

✳

Maybe it's a pasta salad, maybe it's a light entree. Who cares? It's straightforward and bold, without being fussy. And it's fast. This is the kind of pasta that's perfect for an easy weeknight dinner, served hot out of the skillet. But it's primo picnic fare, too. Don't chill it on the way to the picnic site; just let it stay warm. There's a nice duplication in the flavor landscape here: the baby arugula and parsley echo each other. Baby arugula is pretty darn easy to find these days. Look for it with the bagged salads.

SERVES 4 TO 6

8 ounces rotini or other dried pasta with lots of
nooks and crannies

¼ cup olive oil

2 shallots, diced

2 cups loosely packed baby arugula

1 cup crumbled feta (about 4 ounces)

¼ cup dried cranberries

2 tablespoons chopped fresh flatleaf parsley

2 teaspoons lemon juice, or to taste

Salt and pepper to taste

Boil the pasta according to the package instructions until it is al dente, firm to the bite. Drain.

While the pasta cooks, heat the olive oil over medium heat in a large skillet. Sauté the shallots just until they start to brown lightly. Pour the drained pasta into the skillet, then add the remaining ingredients. Toss, off the heat, until everything is nicely combined. Serve immediately if dining at home, or later at room temperature for a picnic.

POTATOES, PEAS, AND CARROTS IN A SPICY TOMATO SAUCE

✳

This humble vegetarian dish comes from northern India, where it—and dishes like it—are favorites served for almost any occasion, including picnics. Serve it in bowls and top it generously with plain yogurt or Mint and Yogurt Cucumber Relish (page 122). The yogurt helps balance out the lively heat and spiciness of the dish. By all means, don't forget the Ginger Iced Tea (page 24). Much of the dish's character comes from the distinctive Indian spice blend called garam masala, which traditionally includes coriander, cumin, cardamom, cinnamon, cloves, and black pepper. Many supermarkets carry garam masala, and it's easy to find in gourmet stores, natural foods stores, and via mail order. Don't substitute curry powder.

SERVES 6

3 tablespoons peanut oil

1 medium onion, finely diced

1-inch-long peeled piece fresh ginger, finely diced

2 medium tomatoes, cored and chopped

1½ teaspoons salt

1½ teaspoons garam masala

¾ teaspoon cayenne pepper

¼ teaspoon turmeric

¼ teaspoon ground coriander

1 pound potatoes, peeled and diced

¾ pound carrots, peeled and diced

1½ cups frozen peas, thawed

In a large nonstick skillet, heat the oil over medium-high heat. When the oil is hot, add the onion and sauté, stirring occasionally, until it begins to brown, about 5 minutes. Stir in the ginger and let it cook for a minute, then add the tomatoes, salt, and spices. Cook and stir the mixture until it thickens somewhat, about 5 minutes.

Stir in the potatoes, carrots, and ⅔ cup water. Bring to a simmer, then cover, reduce the heat to low, and cook until the potatoes and carrots are tender (but not mushy), about 15 minutes. Add the peas and cook for 5 more minutes.

For a picnic, serve at room temperature. For dining at home, or a backyard picnic, you can serve it hot or warm.

CREPES STUFFED WITH CHARD, FETA, PINE NUTS, AND GOLDEN RAISINS

✳

I always *wanted* to be the kind of guy who ate Swiss chard and loved it, but it didn't come about until my girlfriend, Kelly, started cooking chard for me. Sure, it was healthy and hearty, but it tasted fantastic, too. So this recipe, I admit, I swiped almost directly from her, although it was my idea to put it into crepes, which makes it very portable and picnic-y and a bit more special than usual.

MAKES ABOUT 16 CREPES TO SERVE 6 TO 8

CREPES

1 cup all-purpose flour

1 cup milk

2 large eggs

3 tablespoons canola oil, plus oil for greasing

¼ teaspoon salt

Process the ingredients with ⅓ cup water in a blender for 5 seconds. Repeat, then chill the mixture for at least 30 minutes.

When you're ready to cook the crepes, lightly grease a small crepe pan, nonstick skillet, or cast-iron skillet with vegetable oil. Let the skillet warm up over medium heat, then add about 3 tablespoons of batter and quickly tilt the pan around so that the batter coats the bottom. Cook the crepe until it's lightly browned on the bottom, then turn it out onto a paper towel to cool. Make the rest of the crepes this way. Stack the cooled crepes and either use them within a couple of hours or wrap them in plastic wrap and chill them for up to 3 days.

FILLING

3 tablespoons olive oil

1 medium Vidalia or yellow onion

4 garlic cloves

$\frac{1}{8}$ to $\frac{1}{4}$ teaspoon crushed red pepper flakes

Salt and freshly ground black pepper

1 pound Swiss chard, stems removed, cut into 1-inch ribbons

$\frac{1}{4}$ cup pine nuts

$\frac{1}{4}$ cup golden raisins

1 tablespoon lemon juice, or to taste

1 cup crumbled feta cheese (about 4 ounces)

Add the olive oil to a large skillet, then sauté until soft the onion, garlic, red pepper flakes, and salt and pepper to taste. Add the chard, pine nuts, raisins, and lemon juice and continue cooking until the chard is soft, 5 to 10 minutes. Off the heat, stir in the feta. Taste for salt and pepper. Let the mixture cool to lukewarm, then either stuff the crepes (if you plan to serve them within a couple of hours) or chill the chard mixture overnight.

Within a couple hours of serving, put 2 to 3 tablespoons of filling in each crepe and roll the crepes, then arrange them on a serving tray. Serve them at room temperature. They can be refrigerated for 1 day.

ROASTED POBLANO QUICHE WITH QUESO FRESCO

✳

Roasted poblano peppers are so wonderful because of their rich, warm flavor and their friendly level of heat. They look something like dark, skinny green bell peppers, and they're readily available nationwide, year-round. If you've never had them, make this quiche and you'll be a fan for life. The custard of the quiche tempers the heat, so even with the addition of a jalapeño or two this isn't a hot dish. A little dab of Tomatillo Salsa really brings this quiche to life. The crumbly, fetalike queso fresco is also happily common in supermarkets these days.

SERVES 6 TO 8

1 tablespoon olive oil

2 cups chopped scallions

2 poblano peppers, roasted (see page 87), peeled, seeded, and chopped

1 or 2 jalapeño peppers, roasted, peeled, seeded, and chopped, optional

2 tablespoons flour

½ teaspoon salt

Freshly ground black pepper

1 cup crumbled queso fresco or mild feta cheese (about 4 ounces)

1 recipe Whole Wheat Quiche Pastry in a 9-inch pie pan (page 133)

1 cup whole milk

2 large eggs

¼ teaspoon ground cumin, optional

Chopped fresh cilantro

1 recipe Tomatillo Salsa (page 134), optional

Preheat the oven to 375°F.

In a medium skillet over medium heat, heat the olive oil. Sauté the scallions until they're soft and just starting to brown, about 10 minutes. Add the poblanos and jalapeños, if desired, and heat through. Stir in the flour, salt, and pepper, and remove the mixture from the heat.

Layer half of the cheese on the bottom of the quiche crust. Add the pepper mixture. Beat the milk and eggs together and pour them over the quiche. Top with the rest of the cheese and the cumin, if desired.

Bake for 35 to 40 minutes, until the custard is set and the crust is browned. Serve garnished with cilantro and tomatillo salsa, if desired.

For a picnic, serve the quiche at room temperature or cold. Though best the day it's made, it can be refrigerated for 2 days. For dining at home, or a backyard picnic, the dish is also good served warm.

Packing reminder: Bring a pie server.

WHOLE WHEAT
QUICHE PASTRY

✳

The yogurt in this recipe not only keeps the dough tender, but makes it smooth and easy to roll out. This is now my standby savory pastry crust. The butter and whole wheat add just the right amount of flavor. Nonfat, low-fat, and regular yogurt work equally well in this recipe.

MAKES ONE 9-INCH PASTRY

¾ cup whole wheat flour

½ cup all-purpose flour

¼ teaspoon salt

6 tablespoons (¾ stick) chilled unsalted butter, cut into pieces

½ cup plain yogurt

Stir together the flours and salt. Cut in the butter with a pastry cutter (or pinch the butter pieces into the flour) until the largest bits of butter are the size of peas. Stir in the yogurt. Be patient and stir until it starts to clump together in big clumps. Then you can knead it a few times to incorporate any remaining flour.

Pat the dough into a thick disk, wrap it securely in plastic wrap, and chill it for 30 minutes, or up to 24 hours. It can also be frozen at this point—wrapped securely—for up to 2 months.

Roll out the chilled dough on a floured counter and fit it into a standard 9-inch pie pan. Fold the overhanging dough under to form a rim. Cover and chill until needed, for up to 8 hours.

TOMATILLO SALSA

✳

If you've walked past tomatillos—those weird green-tomatoes-in-paper-husk-looking things—in the market and wondered what the heck they're used for, here's one great answer. They make an easy salsa that goes well with so many other flavors. This recipe is my girlfriend Kelly's, and every time I taste it, I'm reminded of the fantastic Mexican meals she's prepared. As you can see from the recipe, there's plenty of room to adjust the amounts of certain ingredients to suit your taste.

MAKES ABOUT 2 CUPS

8 medium tomatillos, husks removed, washed

1 to 2 jalapeño peppers

2 to 3 thick slices of white or yellow onion

2 garlic cloves, left unpeeled

2 to 4 tablespoons freshly squeezed lime juice

½ cup loosely packed fresh cilantro

Salt

Preheat the broiler to high and place the oven rack about 4 inches from the broiler element.

On a baking sheet lined with foil, broil the tomatillos, jalapeños, onions slices, and garlic all at once. As the tomatillos, onions, and jalapeños become charred and blistered, turn them over so they char evenly.

The different ingredients may finish roasting at different times. The tomatillos, jalapeños, and onions are done when they're evenly charred on all sides. The garlic is done when it is light brown and slightly charred. If there are any juices on the baking sheet, reserve them for the next step. Peel the garlic and jalapeños.

Place the tomatillos, onion, garlic, lime juice, cilantro, and any juices from the baking sheet in a food processor and pulse just to chop and combine the ingredients. Don't puree the salsa. Chop the jalapeños and add them to the food processor, removing the seeds if you want less heat in the salsa. You can add a portion of the jalapeños, pulse, then taste to see if you want to add more. Add salt to taste and pulse until the salsa is uniform but not pureed.

Serve at room temperature the same day. Refrigeration will preserve the salsa for a few days, but some of the flavor will fade.

BAKED ONIONS STUFFED WITH FISH AND SPINACH

✳

Here's a light entree in a pleasing (and transportable) package. The contrast between the sweet crunchiness of the baked onion and the buttery mellowness of the spinach is a real delight. Best of all, these can be made a day ahead of time.

MAKES 8 ONIONS

8 medium onions

1 pound flounder, tilapia, cod, or other mild fish

Salt and pepper

9 ounces spinach leaves

6 tablespoons (¾ stick) unsalted butter

¼ cup dry white wine

¼ cup white wine vinegar

Slice the ends off the onions and peel them. Remove any visibly tough or dry outer layers of the onions. With a spoon, hollow out the onions so that the walls are about ¼ inch thick. Try to leave the bottom of each onion intact, but if it comes out, that's okay.

Cut the fish into thin strips. Salt and pepper the strips liberally. Preheat the oven to 325°F and butter a casserole dish large enough to contain the onions.

Wash the spinach, then put it (still wet) in a large pot with 2 tablespoons of the butter. Cover, turn the heat to high, and cook until the spinach is wilted and soft, 2 to 3 minutes. Drain the spinach. Salt it to taste.

Stuff each onion with alternating layers of fish and spinach, ending with spinach on top. Tuck a ½ tablespoon piece of butter into each onion, and drizzle the white wine and white wine vinegar into the onions.

Bake for 1 to 1½ hours, until the onions are semisoft and the fish is cooked. Serve at any temperature.

BEER-BOILED SHRIMP
WITH DILL

✴

These aromatic morsels are addictive. They're also versatile. Make a simple but fantastic sandwich by slathering a soft bun—even a hot dog bun—with good mayonnaise and adding these. Or chop the shrimp and make a simple shrimp salad with mayo and diced celery. You can also sprinkle them on a nice green salad. For a festive backyard picnic, bring the shrimp to the table in the pot and let the guests fish them out themselves. Or let your guests eat them as appetizers, dipped in melted butter and lemon juice. The shrimp are best the day they're made, either warm or at room temperature.

MAKES ENOUGH FOR 4 TO 6 SANDWICHES, OR APPETIZERS FOR 8

2 pounds medium shrimp

2 cans American beer

2 cups loosely packed fresh dill, chopped

2 tablespoons plus 2 teaspoons salt

4 teaspoons caraway seeds

2 teaspoons cracked black peppercorns

1 teaspoon sugar

Freshly squeezed lemon juice, optional

Wash, peel, and devein the shrimp (see Note), putting the shells in a large pot. Add 8 cups water to the pot along with the beer, dill, salt, caraway seeds, peppercorns, and sugar. Bring this mixture to a boil, then add the shrimp. Bring the mixture to a boil again, remove it from the heat, cover, and let sit for 30 minutes to 2 hours. (At this point, you could transport the shrimp to the picnic site in a big thermos jug or other heatproof, watertight container.)

Remove the shrimp from the broth and toss with lemon juice to taste, if desired.

Note: *Small and medium-size shrimp usually don't need to be deveined, as they have little grit in their digestive tracts.*

FLAVORFUL CHICKEN PIECES

✳

Here's a quick and low-fat picnic star that you can't go wrong with. It's a no-fuss recipe. It also packs more flavor than you'd think it could, thanks to the seasoned egg white crust. Versatility is it's strength, too. Chop it and mix it with mayo for an unbeatable chicken salad. Or slice it on the bias and put it on a green salad. It's even good eaten out of hand, like fried chicken, or on fresh bread for a chicken sandwich. It marries especially well with Crisp Green Beans in Jalapeño Oil (page 83) and cold mashed potatoes. Feel free to flavor the recipe however you like. Add some garlic, for instance, or fresh herbs. This recipe is one of those that I call "Friday dinner, Saturday picnic," since it makes a good dinner when hot, and the leftovers make for a great picnic the next day.

SERVES 6

1½ pounds skinless, boneless chicken breasts

4 large egg whites

¼ cup all-purpose flour

2 tablespoons finely grated Parmesan cheese

2 teaspoons sugar

1 teaspoon salt

Freshly ground black pepper

¼ cup peanut oil, for frying

Rinse the chicken and pat it dry. If the breasts are still connected to each other, separate them. Trim the gristle and then cut each breast lengthwise, making 3 long narrow pieces for each breast.

In a bowl, whisk the egg whites. Separately stir together the remaining ingredients (except the oil). Pour the dry ingredients into the egg whites and whisk until the mixture is uniform.

Heat 2 tablespoons of the oil in a large nonstick skillet over medium heat. When the oil is hot, dredge half of the breast pieces in the egg white mixture and put them in the skillet. Cook them until nicely browned on each side, 3 to 5 minutes per side. Some thicker pieces may require additional cooking. Add the remaining 2 tablespoons oil to the pan and cook the remaining chicken.

Serve hot, at room temperature, or cold.

MUSTARDY CHICKEN WINGS

✳

I'm one of those people who can't get enough mustard. It's probably a genetic defect, but I'm not complaining. Humble yellow mustard makes these finger-food chicken wings downright irresistible, but Dijon or brown mustard would work as well. I like these wings hot or warm—so they're perfect for a backyard picnic. Room-temperature wings are nearly as good; if you take them to the picnic cold, they'll be about the right temperature after they sit in the sun for only a few minutes. There's not much meat on these puppies, so make a double batch if needed.

MAKES 16 PIECES TO SERVE 2 OR 3

½ cup yellow mustard

¼ cup extra virgin olive oil

2 tablespoons honey

1 shallot, minced

1 tablespoon chopped fresh flatleaf parsley

½ teaspoon salt, or to taste

Lots of freshly ground black pepper

8 chicken wings (about 1¾ pounds)

Prepare your marinade by combining all the ingredients but the chicken in a large zipper-lock plastic bag.

Rinse the chicken wings and pat them dry. With a heavy chef's knife or cleaver, chop through each of the joints in the wing—i.e., cut each wing into 3 pieces. Discard the wing tips or reserve them for chicken stock.

Put the wings in the bag with the marinade, seal the bag, and shake until the marinade is distributed. Put the bag in the refrigerator for at least 2 hours, or overnight.

Preheat the oven to 450°F. Lightly grease a nonstick baking sheet with butter. Pour the wings and their marinade onto the sheet and spread the wings in one layer.

Bake for 25 to 30 minutes, until the juices run clear and the wings are beginning to brown.

LITTLE MEATBALLS
WITH CHERRIES

✳

While writing this book, I read as many picnic and summery cookbooks as I could find, just to see what other people had done. By far the best book I came across was Claudia Roden's 1981 *Picnic*. It was packed with great recipes, ideas, and an astonishing amount of research. She graciously allowed me to reprint this recipe, which I adore for its simplicity and the clarity of its flavors.

Claudia told me that these days she often uses dried sour cherries for this recipe, since they're available year-round. To substitute dried cherries, use half the amount specified in the recipe, and soak them in water for about 30 minutes before using. Another year-round substitute would be frozen sour cherries, thawed. But to be honest, nothing is quite as good as fresh sour cherries.

Serve the meatballs and cherries with, on, or in pita bread. I like to scoop up the meatballs with the bread.

SERVES 6 TO 8

2 pounds ground lamb or veal

½ teaspoon ground nutmeg

½ teaspoon ground cloves

½ teaspoon ground cinnamon

Salt and freshly ground black pepper

Canola oil, for frying

1 pound pitted sour cherries

Sugar

Freshly squeezed lemon juice

Pita bread

Mix the meat, spices, salt, and pepper with your hands until smooth. Form the meat into marble-size balls, or larger, and fry them over medium heat in a thin layer of oil, turning them to make sure they brown all over.

In a large pan, heat the cherries over medium-high heat, adding sugar or lemon juice to taste. Once the cherries have released their juices, mash them a bit with a fork or potato masher. Add the meatballs and simmer them until they're cooked through and the cherry juice has thickened a bit. If the juice becomes thick before the meatballs are cooked, add water and continue cooking.

For a picnic, serve the meatballs at room temperature or cold. They can be refrigerated for up to 2 days. For dining at home, or a backyard picnic, the meatballs are also good warm (with warm pitas, too).

PHYLLO-CRUSTED PORK AND LEEK PIE

✳

The Greeks are masters of simple savory pies, so I stole some ideas from them for this satisfying dish. It's Mediterranean comfort food at its best—somewhat akin to our meatloaf—and because it's baked in a pie pan, it's pretty easy to transport it to a picnic. Good at any temperature, it's best consumed the day it's baked since the phyllo crust loses its signature crispiness if refrigerated. That's not to say that leftovers aren't great. . . . For a picnic, serve it with a good green salad and your meal is complete.

MAKES ONE 9-INCH PIE TO SERVE 6

2 medium leeks, white and light green parts only, well cleaned and diced

1 small onion, diced

2 tablespoons extra virgin olive oil, plus more for brushing the phyllo sheets

1/2 pound lean ground pork

Salt and freshly ground black pepper

2 large eggs, lightly beaten

10 sheets frozen phyllo dough, thawed

2 cups loosely packed spinach leaves

3/4 cup crumbled feta cheese (about 3 ounces)

In a medium skillet, sauté the leeks and onion in the 2 tablespoons olive oil until they're soft, about 10 minutes. Add the pork and salt and pepper to taste, and cook the pork until it's cooked through, stirring frequently and breaking it into small pieces as it cooks. Let the mixture cool for a few minutes off the heat. If there's a lot of extra liquid, you may want to drain it off. Taste for seasonings, then stir in the eggs.

Preheat the oven to 350°F. Brush the bottom of a 9-inch pie pan lightly with olive oil, then layer 5 sheets of phyllo dough into it, brushing or spraying each one with oil. The dough will hang over the sides.

Fill the pie with the pork mixture, then spread on the spinach and feta. Now layer 5 more sheets of phyllo dough onto the pie, again brushing or spraying each with olive oil. Brush the top of the last sheet with oil, too.

With scissors, trim the phyllo dough so that only about 1 inch overhangs the rim of the pie pan, then tuck that loose flap down between the pie plate and the pie. This will form a bit of a rim on the pie.

Bake the pie for 40 to 50 minutes, until it's lightly browned and fragrant.

For a picnic, serve the pie at room temperature within 1 hour of being baked. It can also be refrigerated for 2 days, though, as already pointed out, this makes the phyllo a bit soggy. For dining at home, or a backyard picnic, the pie is also good warm.

Packing reminder: Bring a pie server.

ONION AND BACON TART

✳

Tarte Flambée, the famous Alsatian onion and bacon tart, is a picnic treat. It's on the rich side, so I think it's best to keep portions small and to serve it with a fresh green salad. A good Riesling is the perfect match. Crème fraîche is a thick cultured cream common in France. Most gourmet stores carry it, but you can find it in many supermarkets, either alongside the cottage cheese or with the other cheeses.

SERVES 4 TO 6

Half a 17.3-ounce package frozen puff pastry

1/2 cup crème fraîche

1/4 cup cottage cheese

Salt and freshly ground black pepper

Fresh thyme, chopped, optional

1 medium white onion, sliced very thin

1 shallot, sliced very thin

4 ounces uncooked bacon, about 5 thin slices, cut into 1/4-inch-wide bits

---

Let the puff pastry thaw at room temperature for about 30 minutes, then unfold it and let it continue to thaw. Preheat the oven to 400°F.

Puree the crème fraîche and cottage cheese in a food processor until smooth. Add salt and pepper to taste. The bacon will add a bit more salt later.

When the puff pastry is malleable, fit it into an 8 × 8-inch glass baking dish. Spread the crème fraîche mixture over the pastry. Sprinkle on some fresh thyme, if desired.

Sprinkle on the onion, shallot, and bacon pieces. Add a bit more salt and pepper, if desired.

Bake the tart for 25 to 35 minutes, until the pastry is puffed and lightly browned and the bacon is cooked.

For a picnic, serve the tart at room temperature or cold. It can be refrigerated for up to 2 days. For dining at home, or a backyard picnic, the tart is also great served warm.

Packing reminder: Bring a pie server.

MAKE YOUR OWN SPRING ROLLS (WITH TWO SAUCES)
A.K.A. "CHOOSE YOUR OWN ADVENTURE SPRING ROLLS"

✳

Any excuse to display my wide array of tiny bowls, custard cups, and ramekins is a good excuse, and if the recipe that uses them is as fun and simple as this one, all the better. The concept is simple: each person picks up a leaf of lettuce, fills it with a mixture of fillings, then drizzles it with a bit of sauce and eats it taco style. How much fun is that for a light picnic? And all those little toppings, arrayed in various bowls! Freaktacular!

The sauces work well individually, but I've discovered that when combined on one spring roll they're even better. I advise preparing them before the main ingredients, since they keep well.

SERVES 4

PEANUT SAUCE

¼ cup smooth peanut butter

1 tablespoon soy sauce

2 teaspoons sugar

2 garlic cloves, minced

½ teaspoon cider vinegar

½ teaspoon Asian chili sauce, optional

Freshly ground black pepper to taste

HOISIN SAUCE

½ onion, finely chopped

2 tablespoons minced fresh peeled ginger

2 tablespoons canola oil

1 tablespoon hoisin sauce
1 tablespoon ketchup
2 teaspoons sugar

1 pound medium shrimp, peeled and deveined
Salt and pepper
2 heads leaf, Bibb, or other medium-leafed lettuce, washed and dried
2 medium cucumbers, peeled, seeded, and cut into thin strips or matchsticks
6 scallions (white and light green parts only), sliced thin
2 carrots, shredded
1 jalapeño pepper, cut into very thin rings
12 or more fresh basil leaves, left whole
12 or more fresh mint leaves, left whole
A handful of fresh cilantro leaves
1 cup unsalted dry-roasted peanuts

For the peanut sauce, whisk the peanut butter with ¼ cup hot water until the mixture is smooth. Vigorously stir in the remaining ingredients. Use immediately or chill for up to 3 days.

For the hoisin sauce, sauté the onion and ginger in the oil over medium-high heat just until the onion starts to brown, 5 to 10 minutes. Add the remaining ingredients and 3 tablespoons water. Stir to combine, then lower the heat and simmer the sauce until it thickens a bit, about 5 minutes.

For the shrimp, bring a medium saucepan of water to a boil, then drop in the peeled shrimp and cook until they're pink, opaque, and just cooked through, about 45 seconds. Drain them, season generously with salt and pepper, and set aside to cool.

Meanwhile, arrange all the other ingredients in appropriate bowls or on trays, etc. Chop the cooled shrimp and put them in a bowl, too. Cover the bowls and transport them to the picnic, keeping them cool if possible.

CHORIZO AND POTATO TACOS
WITH *ESCABECHE*

✳

For something different but not daunting, try the Central Mexican flavors of these picnic-friendly tacos. Think of the tangy, slightly crunchy *escabeche* as kind of a tomatoless salsa—onions, carrots, garlic, and jalapeño in a flavorful vinegar. If you can prepare it a day in advance, the flavors are even more amazing. Heat your tortillas at home and wrap them in towels or foil and they'll keep warm for the trip to the picnic site. Or if you have a grill at your picnic, heat them on it briefly just before filling them. For even less fuss, make these into burritos before leaving home.

SERVES 4

4 tablespoons extra virgin olive oil

1 medium carrot, finely diced

1 jalapeño pepper, seeded and finely diced

1 garlic clove, minced

½ onion, finely diced

⅓ cup cider vinegar

½ teaspoon salt

¼ teaspoon ground allspice

1 bay leaf

1 large potato (¾ pound), peeled and diced

¾ pound Mexican chorizo sausage

Corn or flour tortillas, warm

Plain yogurt

For the *escabeche*, heat 3 tablespoons of the olive oil in a medium skillet over medium heat. Sauté the carrot, jalapeño, and garlic until the carrot is barely tender, about 5 minutes. Stir in the onion, vinegar, salt, allspice, and bay leaf. Remove the mixture from the heat. Chill the *escabeche* if you're not using it within a few hours.

Boil the potato in salted water until tender, about 10 minutes. Drain and reserve.

In a large skillet, heat the remaining 1 tablespoon olive oil over medium heat. Squeeze the sausage out of its casing and fry it until cooked, about 10 minutes, breaking it up into small pieces as it cooks. Remove it from the skillet and reserve.

Fry the potatoes in the hot skillet until they're lightly browned, about 10 minutes, stirring frequently. Add the chorizo and heat through. Taste for salt.

Serve hot, warm, or at room temperature. Remove the bay leaf from the *escabeche* immediately before serving. To make a taco, spoon the chorizo filling into a warm tortilla, then top with *escabeche* and yogurt to taste.

SWEETS GALORE

BISCUITS, BERRIES, HONEY, AND CREAM

✳

This rustic treat is straight from my childhood, and about as good as food gets. I suppose it was my mother's Ozark rendition of strawberries and cream. Whenever you get your hands on some great local berries, try this as a breakfast picnic or as a picnic dessert. I'm partial to strawberries, but whatever's in season will work best. Frozen berries (thawed) make an acceptable wintertime substitution.

SERVES 4 TO 6

1 to 2 quarts berries, cleaned and hulled

Sugar, optional

1 recipe Buttermilk Biscuits (page 110) or Quickest Drop Biscuits (page 157)

Honey

Cream or milk

Before your picnic, if you're using strawberries—especially if they're less than perfect—you may want to cut them up, sprinkle them with sugar, and let them macerate for at least 20 minutes (or as long as it takes you to get to your picnic site . . .). Other berries usually don't need sugar, but a little won't *hurt*. Some people may like a portion of their blueberries or raspberries mashed and sweetened.

At your picnic site, let the guests assemble their own treats in the following way. First, crumble 2 or 3 biscuits in a cereal bowl. Second, add as many berries as you desire. Then drizzle on the honey. And finally add a small portion of cream or milk—but not so much that the berries are swimming.

Eat immediately. Repeat.

QUICKEST DROP BISCUITS

✳

Got some berries on hand but don't want to mess with a fussy biscuit recipe? You can have these out of the oven in 20 minutes, start to finish. For something special to go with berries, add the grated zest of one orange to the batter.

MAKES 16 SMALL BISCUITS

2 cups all-purpose flour

2½ teaspoons baking powder

1 teaspoon salt

¼ cup peanut or canola oil

1 cup milk

Preheat the oven to 450°F. Lightly grease 2 baking sheets with nonstick cooking spray.

Sift the dry ingredients into a bowl. Add the oil and milk and stir just until the dry ingredients are incorporated.

Drop heaping spoonfuls of the batter onto the prepared baking sheets and bake for 8 to 12 minutes, until lightly browned on the bottom. Use them as described in Biscuits, Berries, Honey, and Cream (page 156).

SOUR CHERRY MINI-CRUMBLES

✳

Sour (or tart) cherries are like little parcels of summer, and I can't resist their puckery brightness. But for whatever reason, sweet cherries are much easier to find. Is it some kind of plot? Sweet cherries often don't taste like anything. Luckily, even those of us who never see fresh sour cherries can usually find them in the freezer section of the supermarket. These mini-crumbles are easy to transport and good at any temperature. Serve with ice cream, crème anglaise, yogurt, or high-quality cream.

MAKES 6 MINI-CRUMBLES

¼ cup plus 1 tablespoon all-purpose flour

¼ cup packed light brown sugar

Pinch of salt

4 tablespoons (½ stick) chilled unsalted butter, cut into pieces

¼ cup raw walnuts, finely chopped

1 pound frozen pitted tart cherries

⅓ cup granulated sugar

½ teaspoon finely grated lemon zest

½ teaspoon vanilla extract

Preheat the oven to 375°F. Butter six 4- to 6-ounce ramekins or custard cups and set them on a baking sheet.

Prepare the crumble topping first. Combine 3 tablespoons of the flour, the brown sugar, and the salt. Cut in the butter until the mixture is crumbly. Stir in the walnuts.

Separately combine the cherries, sugar, lemon zest, vanilla, and the remaining 2 tablespoons flour. This mixture won't really come together—just toss it as well as you can. There will be a loose sugar mixture at the bottom of the bowl.

Spoon the cherry mixture into the ramekins, trying to give each ramekin equal amounts of cherries and the loose sugar mixture. Top each ramekin with the crumble mixture and bake for 24 to 30 minutes, until bubbly and browned.

For a picnic, serve the mini-crumbles at room temperature. Beforehand, they can be refrigerated for up to 3 days. For dining at home, or a backyard picnic, the crumbles are great served warm.

HONEY MACAROONS

✳

Forget all that brainwashing about coconut being bad for you. It turns out that coconut oil may be one of the most healthy fats on the planet. Decide for yourself. These soft and petite cookies are like tiny portions of sunshine. Think about it: honey is made of pollen from flowers that worship the sun. And coconut evokes the sunny tropics where it grows. These cookies keep well at room temperature, and get softer each day.

MAKES ABOUT 40 SMALL MACAROONS
2¼ cups finely shredded unsweetened coconut (see Note)

scant ½ cup honey

3 large egg whites

Preheat the oven to 325°F. Line 2 baking sheets with parchment paper.

Combine the ingredients in a large saucepan and stir over medium heat until the mixture steams for about a minute. Remove from the heat and drop 2-teaspoon portions onto the baking sheets. Smooth the macaroons with your fingertips, if desired.

Bake for 12 to 16 minutes, until lightly browned and fragrant. Slide the parchment paper with the macaroons off the sheets and onto a cooling rack.

Note: *Shredded unsweetened coconut, often labeled as "desiccated" coconut, is available at bulk foods stores and natural foods stores. Make sure it's finely shredded, with flakes much smaller than grains of rice. Also, don't make the mistake of buying the sweetened shredded coconut you commonly see in supermarkets.*

RHUBARB CUSTARD TART

✳

The springtime tartness of rhubarb and the creamy mellowness of a brown sugar custard are an ideal match. Any tart this good should probably be regulated by the government. Or at least taxed. And the best part is that it's a true no-fuss recipe. But when the last piece is gone, it's a fair bet that there'll be fussing aplenty.

MAKES ONE 9-INCH TART TO SERVE 6 TO 8

1 unbaked Five-Minute Tart Crust (page 165), fitted into
a 9-inch tart pan with a removable bottom

1¾ cups rhubarb in ¼-inch dice

¾ cup packed light brown sugar

1 tablespoon flour

1 large egg

1 large egg yolk

½ cup milk

½ teaspoon vanilla extract

Preheat the oven to 375°F. Place the tart pan with crust on a sturdy baking sheet.

Spread the rhubarb in the unbaked crust. Separately combine the remaining ingredients and whisk until the mixture is smooth. Pour it over the rhubarb.

Bake the tart on the baking sheet for 25 to 35 minutes, just until set. If you notice any large bubbles lifting up the custard as it bakes, you can deflate them with the tip of a knife. Let it cool on a wire rack. Serve it at room temperature or chilled. It can be refrigerated for up to 3 days.

Packing reminder: Bring a pie server.

LEMON-BLUEBERRY
CUSTARD TART

✳

This classic tart is a picnic favorite. My rendition is easier to make than most lemon-blueberry tarts because I skip the whole business of making a lemon curd. Why shouldn't the custard and blueberries simply cook together in the oven?

Great fresh, this tart is even better if it is refrigerated overnight so that the flavors can meld. Serve it cold, if possible. It can be refrigerated for up to 3 days. Of course, fresh local blueberries make the best tart, but frozen blueberries work just fine.

SERVES 6 TO 8

1 unbaked Five-Minute Tart Crust (page 165), fitted into
a 9-inch tart pan with a removable bottom

1¾ cups fresh or frozen blueberries, thawed

⅔ cup sugar

1 tablespoon all-purpose flour

1 large egg

1 large egg yolk

½ cup milk

2 teaspoons lemon juice

½ teaspoon grated lemon zest, or more to taste

Follow the directions for Rhubarb Custard Tart (page 161), substituting the blueberries for the rhubarb.

Packing reminder: Bring a pie server.

BUTTERMILK-PEACH TART

✴

The tanginess of the buttermilk is a nice counterpoint to the warm sweetness of the peaches.

SERVES 6 TO 8

1 unbaked Five-Minute Tart Crust (page 165), fitted into
a 9-inch tart pan with a removable bottom

3 medium peaches

½ cup packed light brown sugar

1 tablespoon all-purpose flour

1 large egg

1 large egg yolk

½ cup buttermilk

¼ teaspoon cinnamon

Bring a pot of water to a boil. Boil the peaches for 30 seconds, then immediately place them in a bowl of ice water. Peel the peaches, then slice them into thin wedges and spread the wedges in the tart crust.

Follow the directions for Rhubarb Custard Tart (page 161). Serve cold. It can be refrigerated for up to 3 days.

Packing reminder: Bring a pie server.

FIVE-MINUTE TART CRUST

✴

This beyond-tender, supremely crumbly, tiny-bit-sweet tart crust will become your new best friend. When your guests praise it (and praise it they will), don't admit that it only took a few minutes to create: make up a French-sounding name for it and tell them you've been working on the technique for seven years.

My aunt Lucretia first told me about this kind of crust. She uses it as a piecrust. See the variation below.

MAKES ONE 9-INCH TART CRUST

6 tablespoons (¾ stick) unsalted butter
¾ cup plus 2 tablespoons all-purpose flour
1½ tablespoons confectioners' sugar
Pinch of salt

Melt the butter in a bowl in the microwave. Add the flour, sugar, and salt and stir with a fork until the mixture is smooth and clumps together. Immediately put the crust in a 9-inch tart pan. With your fingers, press the crust into the pan and up the sides, being careful to patch any holes.

If your recipe calls for a prebaked tart shell, line the shell with foil, fill it with dry beans or rice, and bake the crust in a 325°F oven until it browns lightly, about 30 minutes.

FIVE-MINUTE PIECRUST

MAKES ONE 9-INCH PIECRUST

8 tablespoons (1 stick) unsalted butter

1 cup plus 2 tablespoons all-purpose flour

2 tablespoons confectioners' sugar

$\frac{1}{8}$ teaspoon salt

Follow the directions for the Five-Minute Tart Crust and fit the crust into a 9-inch glass pie pan.

IN-THE-PAN CHOCOLATE CAKE

✳

Have cake, will travel. You can transport and serve this simple but satisfying cake in the same pan you bake it in. Throw some aluminum foil over the pan and it'll protect the icing, too. It's a moist and chocolately cake, with a nice warmth added by a teaspoon of cinnamon. The simple chocolate-glaze frosting will remind you of childhood birthday cakes. I got this recipe from my sister's husband's mother, Jackie Luce, who is a terrific home baker. It's an easy cake to make the morning of a picnic. Just don't forget to bring vanilla ice cream, which will be beautifully soft and melty by the time you serve it.

**MAKES ONE 9 × 13-INCH CAKE TO SERVE 12
(FOR A SMALLER RECIPE: A HALF RECIPE FITS IN A
9-INCH ROUND CAKE PAN OR AN 8 × 8-INCH PAN)**

CAKE

12 tablespoons (1½ sticks) butter or regular margarine (see Note)

¼ cup Dutch-process cocoa powder

2 cups all-purpose flour

2 cups sugar

1 teaspoon baking soda

1 teaspoon cinnamon

2 large eggs

½ cup buttermilk

FROSTING

1 cup minus 1 tablespoon confectioners' sugar

1 tablespoon Dutch-process cocoa powder

2 tablespoons buttermilk

2 tablespoons regular margarine

Preheat the oven to 400°F. Butter a nonstick 9 × 13-inch pan.

For the cake, combine the butter or margarine and cocoa powder with 1 cup water in a saucepan. Bring the mixture to a boil, stirring a few times to break up the clumps of cocoa. Remove from the heat.

Sift the flour, sugar, baking soda, and cinnamon into a large bowl. Stir in the hot cocoa mixture until smooth. Whisk in the eggs and buttermilk until the mixture is smooth and uniform. The batter will be thin. Pour the batter into the pan and bake for 18 to 22 minutes, until a toothpick inserted near the middle comes out clean. Set the pan on a wire rack to cool.

To prepare the frosting, stir together the confectioners' sugar and cocoa in a bowl. Bring the buttermilk and margarine to a boil in a small saucepan (or in the microwave), then pour it into the sugar-cocoa mixture and whisk until smooth. Immediately spread the icing onto the cake. Store the cake, covered, at room temperature for up to 3 days.

Note: *Margarine seems to make the moistest cake, but make sure you use regular margarine, not low fat or whipped or some such. I prefer to use butter because it doesn't contain trans fats. If you use unsalted butter, add ¾ teaspoon salt to the dry ingredients.*

BANANA PUDDING

✳

When I went to the National Cornbread Festival in South Pittsburg, Tennessee, in 2003, I was introduced to banana pudding, which is a specialty of the South. I don't know why in the world I'd never had it—or even heard of it—before. When I served it at a family reunion recently, my sister Elizabeth suggested that it should come with a warning label. That's how good it is. Among its lovely attributes are the ease of preparation and the fact that it's actually better the second day. Normally, I'm not one for instant vanilla pudding (and its artificial flavor), but it works in this recipe.

SERVES 6 TO 8

One 3.4-ounce box instant vanilla pudding

2 cups milk

1 cup heavy cream

1 teaspoon sugar

½ teaspoon vanilla extract

6 ounces vanilla wafer cookies (half a 12-ounce box)

3 ripe bananas, sliced into thin rounds

Make the pudding with the milk, following the directions on the package. Whip the cream with the sugar and vanilla until it forms stiff peaks. Fold about half of the whipped cream into the pudding.

Line the bottom of a medium serving bowl or small casserole dish with half of the vanilla wafer cookies. Add a layer of half the banana slices and top with half the pudding. Repeat the layers, then spread the remaining whipped cream on top. If you have any cookies that didn't fit into the layers, crumble them and sprinkle them on top. Cover tightly and chill for at least 3 hours or as long as 2 days. Serve cold.

STRAWBERRY CUPCAKES

✳

My grandmother Jackson was a superb cook and baker, second to none. She made soft dinner rolls that I've still not tasted the equal of. Family members still make some of her excellent Christmas cookies each year. And her lemon meringue pie was so good that each week at the church potluck the first eight people in line got slices of the pie, and then it was gone. Good thing it was a church, or there probably would have been scuffles.

For years, a family in her small town paid her to bake a strawberry cake for them each week. Recently, my aunt found Grandma's recipe for the fabled strawberry cake and I was disappointed to see that it was a cake mix recipe that included a box of strawberry Jell-O. I tested the recipe, and it was truly fantastic, but the neon red color, extreme sweetness, and artificial strawberry flavor were just a bit too much for me. So I set out to develop a recipe that was similar in spirit, but with an ingredients list I could feel better about.

The result—these cupcakes—was a pleasant surprise. Soft and just sweet enough, these cupcakes are real crowd-pleasers. Their pink (not artificial) icing makes them so pretty. I relied on frozen berries in the recipe because they're available year-round and are better and cheaper than the woody, bland berries trucked in from California. (And when good local strawberries are in season, I prefer to use them in a simpler recipe where their flavor can really shine through.)

Cupcakes transport well, but these need to be kept at room temperature or colder to prevent their icing from liquifying. And the icing is where a lot of the berry flavor is. The cupcakes also freeze well, and would probably thaw to the perfect temperature by the time they're served at a picnic.

Yes, at the recipe's end, you're left with about ¼ cup strawberry puree. Mea culpa. So stir it into your yogurt. Can't complain about that.

MAKES 12 CUPCAKES

One 10-ounce package frozen sliced strawberries in syrup, thawed

2 large eggs

1 large egg yolk

1 teaspoon vanilla extract

1¼ cups cake flour

1 cup granulated sugar

1¼ teaspoons baking powder

½ teaspoon salt

½ cup canola or vegetable oil

½ pound (1¾ cups plus 2 tablespoons) confectioners' sugar

2 tablespoons unsalted butter, softened

Preheat the oven to 350°F. Line a standard muffin tin with 12 paper cupcake liners.

Puree the thawed strawberries and their syrup in a blender. Briefly whisk together in a bowl the eggs, egg yolk, vanilla extract, and half the strawberry puree (about ½ cup plus 2 tablespoons).

Separately sift the cake flour, sugar, baking powder, and salt into a mixing bowl. Add the oil and beat with a handheld mixer on medium speed for 2 minutes. Scrape down the bowl, add a third of the strawberry mixture, and beat for another 20 seconds. Repeat twice with the remaining strawberry mixture.

Divide the batter among the 12 cupcake liners and bake the cupcakes for 14 to 20 minutes, just until their tops are softly set and a toothpick inserted in the middle of a cupcake comes up covered with moist crumbs. (Overbaking the cupcakes makes them tough.) Let the cupcakes cool.

Make the icing by beating the confectioners' sugar with the softened butter and about half of the remaining strawberry puree—or enough to make a smooth but not too thin icing. Spread the icing on the cooled cupcakes.

Store the cupcakes, covered, at room temperature for up to 3 days. Or refrigerate or freeze them for longer storage.

TOMORROW COOKIES

✳

In my second novel, *In Summer,* there's a scene at a county fair where the characters are looking at the baking contest entries and see an empty table with a sign that reads "Tomorrow Cookies"—meaning that the cookies will be judged and displayed tomorrow. But one of the characters likes the idea that there are cookies called Tomorrow Cookies and she takes it on herself to invent them. In the book her cookies are described as buttery and tender, with the flavors of orange, almond, and brown sugar. The other characters rave about them, they're so good.

Well, I'd never developed a recipe based on a fictional cookie before, but my first attempt with these turned out a true masterpiece. Now I understand why my characters loved them so much.

MAKES ABOUT 50 COOKIES

1 cup raw almonds

2 oranges

½ pound (2 sticks) unsalted butter, at room temperature

½ cup packed light brown sugar

2 teaspoons vanilla extract

¼ teaspoon salt

2¼ cups all-purpose flour

Confectioners' sugar, for dredging

Process the almonds in a blender or food processor until they are ground to about the consistency of coarse cornmeal. (If using a blender, you may have to scrape down the sides and shake the canister a few times to facilitate even grinding.) Working over the open blender or food processor, zest the oranges, and squeeze and reserve the juice from one orange. Pulse the zest with the ground almonds a few times to distribute and chop the zest.

Using a stand mixer or a strong handheld mixer, beat the butter, brown sugar, vanilla, and salt until the mixture is smooth, 1 to 2 minutes. Add half of the flour and beat on low until the flour is incorporated and the dough clumps together. Beat in 1 teaspoon juice from the orange, then beat in the remaining flour and all the nut mixture. The dough will form small clumps. Knead it a few times by hand to make it a cohesive mass. Wrap the dough in plastic wrap and refrigerate for at least 1 hour or for as long as 3 days.

When you're ready to bake the cookies, line 2 baking sheets with parchment paper and preheat the oven to 350°F. Roll the chilled dough into 1-inch-diameter balls and place them 2 inches apart on the parchment paper.

Bake the cookies for 14 to 16 minutes, until they're lightly browned on the bottom and softly set. Let them cool for a few minutes on the sheet before removing them.

While the cookies are still slightly warm, carefully roll them in a bowl of confectioners' sugar until they are coated. They keep well at room temperature, covered, for 7 days.

SPICY CHAI ICE CREAM

✳

A decidedly decadent cousin of its namesake drink, this ice cream's bouquet of spices is a lovely foil to its cold, creamy texture and touch-of-honey sweetness. Think of it as a summery, picnic-y version of an after-dinner coffee—it soothes the palate and comforts the soul. Experiment with different teas to find your favorite.

To keep ice cream cold for a picnic, wrap its container in a double thickness of foil, then wrap it in towels and put it in a cooler. It may soften a bit, but what's wrong with soft ice cream? Nothin'. Or follow the old-fashioned tradition and churn the ice cream at the picnic.

MAKES ABOUT 5 CUPS

3 cups milk

1 cup heavy cream

¼ cup plus 2 tablespoons honey

¼ cup Assam, jasmine, Darjeeling, or other black loose-leaf tea

2-inch-long piece peeled fresh ginger, thinly sliced

1 or 2 cinnamon sticks

20 whole black peppercorns

12 whole cloves

12 whole green cardamom pods

10 large egg yolks

½ cup sugar

½ teaspoon vanilla extract

Pinch of salt

Bring the milk, cream, honey, tea, ginger, cinnamon, peppercorns, cloves, and cardamom pods to a simmer in a saucepan. Watch the pot carefully to avoid a boil-over. Remove from the heat, cover, and let steep for 5 minutes. Strain the mixture through a fine-mesh sieve.

In a metal bowl or the top of a double-boiler, whisk together the egg yolks and sugar until they thicken and turn pale. Very slowly drizzle in the hot mixture, whisking constantly.

Cook the mixture over simmering water, stirring constantly, until it thickens enough to coat the back of a wooden spoon—7 to 10 minutes. Stir in the vanilla and salt.

Allow the custard to cool to room temperature, then refrigerate it for at least 4 hours or overnight. Prepare the ice cream according to your ice cream maker's directions.

When the ice cream is ready, you can serve it immediately if you want soft ice cream. For a thicker, more commercial-style ice cream, and one that travels well, transfer the ice cream to a freezer-safe container and freeze for 2 or more hours.

Packing reminder: Bring an ice cream scoop.

DUTCH LETTERS

✳

Not far from where I live in Iowa, there's an extraordinarily pretty little town named Pella that retains a lot of the customs and character of its Dutch settlers, including these almond paste and puff pastry treats. They used to be a Christmastime treat, which explains why they're almost always shaped into the letter *S* for Santa Claus, but now they're enjoyed year-round. And thank goodness for that.

MAKES 12

8 ounces almond paste

¼ cup granulated sugar

2 tablespoons light brown sugar

1 egg white

¼ teaspoon vanilla extract

1 sheet puff pastry (half a 17.3-ounce package), thawed

Combine the almond paste, granulated sugar, brown sugar, egg white, and vanilla in a food processor and pulse until the mixture is smooth and uniform. (You can mix by hand, too, mashing the paste with the back of a spoon, but it takes a while.) Refrigerate the mixture for an hour or more, until it's firm.

On a floured counter, cut the puff pastry in half, then roll each half to measure about 10 × 12 inches. Cut six 10 × 2-inch strips from each half.

Preheat the oven to 375°F.

For each piece of puff pastry, roll the chilled almond paste mixture between your palms to make a rope smaller than the diameter of a dime and as long as the puff pastry. Don't worry about making a uniform rope with no breaks. Put the rope down the center of each piece of puff pastry, then fold the pastry around, enclosing the almond paste in a tube of puff pastry. Shape each tube into a big *S* or other letter—keeping the seam side down—and place on an ungreased baking sheet.

Bake six letters per sheet for 16 to 22 minutes—just until lightly browned and puffed. Cool on a wire rack. The letters are best the day they're made, or they can be kept in an airtight container for a few days. They also freeze well—and they'll thaw by the time you reach your picnic site.

YOUR NEW FAVORITE YOGURT

✳

A yogurt to call your own. Homemade yogurt is naturally fresher than anything you can buy in the store, and it isn't loaded with sugar or thickeners. The best part is that it's easier to make than you probably think. You can make this recipe with just milk, but the cream makes it special; it also means a small portion will satisfy you. Sure, it's perfect for a picnic breakfast, but it also makes an unbeatable dessert, or a wonderful topping for soups. As for mix-ins, use your imagination for simple picnic fare: maple syrup, jam, berries, honey, vanilla, etc.

MAKES ABOUT 2 CUPS

1⅓ cups whole milk

⅔ cup heavy cream, preferably pasteurized

(not ultra-pasteurized)

¼ cup plain yogurt with active cultures

Find a warm place in your house—such as you would use when letting bread dough rise—and set a 2-cup-plus container there to warm up.

Meanwhile, heat the milk and cream in a saucepan just until they boil. Watch carefully to avoid a boil-over. Remove the mixture from the heat and let it cool to 110° to 120°F—slightly cooler than hot tap water. Whisk in the yogurt and strain it. Pour the mixture into the container that you've set in a warm place.

Cover the container with an airtight lid (or plastic wrap) and leave it in the warm spot for 8 to 10 hours. Check the mixture's consistency. If it's nicely thickened, but still quite liquid, it's done. If it seems thin, let it sit for another hour and check again. Keep in mind it probably won't be as thick as commercial yogurt.

Cover and refrigerate the yogurt for up to 7 days.

PUFF PASTRY PRUNE PINWHEELS

✳

I tried and tried to come up with a title that wasn't chock-full of al-literation, but I failed. Pillowy Dried-Plum Windmills? Nope. Any-hoo, titles have very little to do with how a recipe tastes, and these taste great. They're a breeze to make, too, and keep well at room temperature for days. In fact, I think they're a little bit better on the second and third days. I like the fact that they're not too sweet.

MAKES ABOUT 30 COOKIES

⅞ cup bite-size pitted prunes (about 4 ounces)

¼ cup packed light brown sugar

1 tablespoon Frangelico liqueur, or other nut liqueur

1 teaspoon grated lemon zest

1 teaspoon all-purpose flour

½ teaspoon vanilla extract

¼ teaspoon ground cinnamon

1 sheet frozen puff pastry (half a 17.3-ounce package), thawed

1 egg, beaten

Combine the prunes, brown sugar, liqueur, lemon zest, flour, vanilla, cin-namon, and 3 tablespoons water in a small saucepan. Cook over medium heat, stirring occasionally, until the liquid is thickened and bubbly, 3 to 5 minutes. Let the mixture cool slightly off the heat, then puree it in a food processor.

Cut the pastry sheet in half lengthwise, making two 9-inch-long rectan-gles. Put half of the prune mixture on one sheet and spread it evenly, leaving a 1-inch border along one of the long sides. Brush the border with the beaten egg and roll the sheet up like a carpet, starting with the side opposite the egg-wash border. Wrap the cookie roll tightly in foil. Repeat with the second pastry sheet. Refrigerate the rolls for at least 3 hours, or up to 2 days.

When you're ready to bake the cookies, preheat the oven to 400°F. Line one large baking sheet with parchment paper. Remove the cookie rolls from their foil and cut them into ½-inch slices. Place the slices—pinwheel side up—on the baking sheet, spacing them 1 inch apart. Bake for 15 to 20 minutes, until the puff pastry is light golden. Slide the cookies onto a rack to cool. The cookies keep in an airtight container for up to a week.

SCRAP-TOP RASPBERRY PIE

✳

After tasting this pie, you'll wonder why raspberry pie isn't as popular as apple, cherry, or blueberry pie. Maybe it's just that raspberry pie is harder to find. True, good fresh raspberries can be hard to come by, but the frozen ones are usually pretty darn good. When they're in season locally, I pick as many as I can and freeze them myself. What could be more welcome than a raspberry pie in February? (Other than a fresh raspberry pie served for a weekend picnic during berry season, that is.)

Sometimes I feel that the top crusts on fruit pies are too thick and bland. And who has time to mess with a lattice top? Solution: trim the scraps from the bottom crust, roll them thin, and then layer them on top of the pie and sprinkle them with sugar. Quick, crisp, lazy.

MAKES ONE 9-INCH PIE TO SERVE 8

1 recipe Sour Cream Piecrust (page 186)

5 cups fresh or frozen raspberries

½ cup granulated sugar, plus more for sprinkling

¼ cup dark brown sugar

3 tablespoons cornstarch

2 tablespoons crème de cassis, framboise, or other dark berry liqueur

1 teaspoon freshly squeezed lemon juice

1 teaspoon vanilla extract

Pinch of salt

Preheat the oven to 400°F.

Roll the chilled crust on a floured work surface until it is about 15 inches in diameter. Lay a pie plate upside down on the crust and cut a circle of crust about 2 inches larger than the pie plate. Fit the crust into the plate and form a rim. Roll the leftover scraps of crust very thin.

Toss all the remaining ingredients until well combined, being careful not to break up the raspberries too much (if you're using fresh berries). Pour the berry mixture into the piecrust, then arrange the crust scraps on top. Sprinkle the top crust with a little sugar.

Put the pie on a baking sheet and bake it for 50 to 60 minutes, until the crust is nicely browned and the filling is very bubbly at the edges. (If using frozen berries, this could take an additional 15 to 20 minutes.)

Serve the pie warm, at room temperature, or chilled, with vanilla ice cream.

Packing reminder: Bring a pie server.

SCRAP-TOP RASPBERRY COBBLER

✳ Whenever I make pies, I keep the little bits of trimmed unbaked piecrust and freeze them. For a quick weeknight cobbler, I make the pie filling above, put it in an 8 × 8 glass baking dish, cover it with the frozen scraps of crust, and sprinkle it with sugar. You can also halve the filling recipe and make 4 to 6 individual cobblers in ramekins (for which the baking time can be reduced to about 30 minutes).

SOUR CREAM PIECRUST

✳

For sweet pies like Scrap-Top Raspberry Pie (page 184), I use this variation of Whole Wheat Quiche Pastry for an easy, flavorful, and tender crust. Make sure you form a solid rim of crust around the lip of the pie pan, as this dough has a tendency to slump.

MAKES ONE 9-INCH PIECRUST

1¼ cups all-purpose flour

1 teaspoon sugar

¼ teaspoon salt

6 tablespoons (¾ stick) unsalted butter, chilled, in pieces

½ cup sour cream

Follow the directions for Whole Wheat Quiche Pastry (page 133), adding the sugar along with the salt and substituting the sour cream for the yogurt.

LITTLE CHOCOLATE COOKIES

✳

Ⅰn a day and age when so many cookies are huge or gooey or full of chunks of something, these two-bite, sugar-crowned morsels are downright refreshing. They're modest and unassuming, straightforward and simple. They're also a bit addictive. The day after I first made them, my girlfriend came out of the kitchen and said to me, "I just ate ten of your damn chocolate cookies." So that's their other name: My Damn Chocolate Cookies.

MAKES 60 TO 70 COOKIES

3 ounces bittersweet chocolate, chopped

12 tablespoons (1½ sticks) unsalted butter, softened

½ cup plus 3 tablespoons sugar, plus more for tops

2 teaspoons vanilla extract

1 large egg

2¼ cups all-purpose flour

1¼ teaspoons baking powder

¼ teaspoon salt

Microwave the chocolate at 50 percent power for 2 minutes. Stir, then heat another 30 seconds. Stir again. Repeat until the chocolate is smooth.

With an electric mixer, beat the butter and sugar together in a mixing bowl until airy, about 5 minutes. On low speed, beat in the chocolate and vanilla. Then beat in the egg until the mixture is uniform.

Separately sift together the flour, baking powder, and salt. Beat these dry ingredients into the wet mixture on low speed until the dough is uniform and there are no bits of flour visible. Cover and chill the dough for at least an hour, or up to 3 days.

When you're ready to bake the cookies, preheat the oven to 375°F. Line 2 silver-colored baking sheets (see Note) with parchment paper.

Roll the dough into balls about the diameter of a quarter, then flatten them slightly. Dip the balls in sugar, then place them sugar side up on the baking sheets, spaced 1½ inches apart. They don't spread much during baking.

Bake the cookies for 7 to 10 minutes, until they're softly set and their tops are cracked. Cool on the baking sheets briefly before cooling completely on a wire rack. The cookies keep well, covered, at room temperature for 5 days.

Note: *These damn chocolate cookies are a bit prone to burning on the bottom, so it's best to use silver-colored baking sheets. If you only have gray or black baking sheets, pull the cookies out of the oven a minute or two early.*

JULY FRUIT SALAD

✳

Yay for July! That most summery of summer months. The blue-berries come at the start of the month, the peaches arrive in the middle, and the raspberries close it out. Serve this juicy fruit salad straight up or with ice cream and Simple Yogurt Cake (page 198).

SERVES 6

4 peaches

1 cup blueberries

2 tablespoons freshly squeezed lime juice, or to taste

Pure maple syrup

2/3 cup raspberries

Put the peaches into boiling water for 30 seconds, then immediately cool them off in a bowl of ice water. Peel them and cut into segments.

Toss the peaches with the blueberries, lime juice, and maple syrup to taste. The idea with the maple syrup is to add a bit of sweetness with a haunting background flavor—don't overdo it.

Gently stir in the raspberries. Serve immediately or chill for up to several hours.

APPLE CIDER TARTLETTES

✳

For the settlers in the central and western United States, refined sugar was a luxury. So they relied on natural sweeteners, like honey or maple syrup. One trick was to boil down apple cider until it was extra sweet and syrupy, and then make a pie with the syrup. Concentrated cider is breathtakingly tangy and intense, so I think little tartlettes—with their higher ratio of crust to filling—are better than pie. Top them with whipped cream or Mexican *crema*. You can transport them in their tartlette pans to protect them.

MAKES SIX 4-INCH TARTLETTES

One recipe Five-Minute Piecrust (page 166),
fitted into six 4-inch tartlette pans

3 cups fresh apple cider

1 large egg

¼ teaspoon vanilla extract

Dash of cinnamon

Dash of salt

Preheat the oven to 325°F. Line the tartlette pans with foil and fill them with dry beans or rice. Bake the tartlette shells on a baking sheet for 30 minutes. Let cool.

Raise the oven temperature to 350°F.

Boil the apple cider until it is reduced to ¾ cup. Let it cool somewhat, then whisk in the remaining ingredients and divide the mixture among the 6 tartlette shells.

Bake the tartlettes on a baking sheet for 14 to 16 minutes, until just set.

For a picnic, serve at room temperature or cold. The tarts can be refrigerated for up to 3 days. For dining at home, or a backyard picnic, the tarts are also good warm.

CHERRY-BERRY PICKLED PINEAPPLES

✳

Yes, you can pickle fruit, and it's a glorious thing: tangy and sweet and bold. It's really just a way of intensifying the flavors and preserving the fruit at the same time. This pickled pineapple is powerful stuff, fortified with berry, cherry, and lime flavors. Unless you're looking for a stomachache, you wouldn't really want to eat a whole bowl of it. But sprinkle it in a fruit salad for a tremendous boost. Or eat a little of it with ice cream, a nice buttery pound cake, or Simple Yogurt Cake (page 198). The tart, berrylicious, vanilla-infused pickling juice also can be used very sparingly, drizzled on any of the things you would serve the pineapple on: fruit salad, ice cream, cake.

I've scaled this recipe for half a pineapple because a little bit goes a long way. Just eat the other half of the pineapple fresh.

MAKES 2½ CUPS

½ vanilla bean

½ cup raspberry vinegar

⅓ cup sour cherry juice (see Note)

2 tablespoons light brown sugar

Juice and grated zest of ½ lime

½ fresh pineapple, peeled, cored, and cut into medium-size bits

---

Slice the vanilla bean lengthwise and scrape the little seeds into a medium nonreactive pan. Add the bean pod, too, as well as all the ingredients except the pineapple. Bring the mixture to a boil, stirring to dissolve the sugar. Lower the heat and simmer for 10 minutes. Let the mixture cool to lukewarm or cooler, remove the vanilla bean pod, then pour the mixture over the pineapple bits.

Chill the pineapple in the juice for 24 hours before using. Refrigerated, the pineapple keeps for 2 weeks or more.

Note: *Sour cherry juice isn't that hard to find these days. Check a good natural foods store if your supermarket doesn't have it. Or substitute another juice.*

PERFECT PEACH
ICE CREAM

✳

The tradition of making ice cream at picnics has been around for more than a century now, and I would hate to think it's fading away. This recipe is ideal for on-site ice cream churning, whether you've got an old-fashioned crank-and-salt machine or a handy electrical outlet for a newer machine. When freshly churned, this ice cream is soft and peachy and, well, perfect. As far as I'm concerned, peach is one of those flavors that commercial ice cream makers just can't seem to get right, which is another reason to do it yourself. But wait till the really good peaches arrive—don't waste your time with the off-season supermarket variety.

You also can make this ice cream ahead of time, no problem. Stored overnight in the freezer, it becomes harder, more like a commercial-style ice cream.

To keep the ice cream frozen during transport, wrap its container in a layer or two of foil, then wrap it in towels and put it in a cooler.

MAKES ABOUT 2 QUARTS

6 ripe medium peaches

2/3 cup granulated sugar

2 vanilla beans

1 1/3 cups milk

2 cups cream

2 large eggs

4 large egg yolks

1/2 cup light brown sugar

Pinch of salt

1 cup sour cream
2 teaspoons Grand Marnier, optional

On a coarse cheese grater, grate the peaches into a bowl, being sure to catch their pulp and juices. Most of the skin won't go through the grater, but it's okay if some does. Stir in the granulated sugar (but not the brown sugar) and refrigerate until needed.

Split the vanilla beans and scrape their tiny seeds into a small saucepan. Add the bean pods, the milk, and 1 cup of the cream. Heat the mixture over medium-high heat just until small bubbles and steam begin to rise. Remove the milk from the heat, cover, and let steep for 10 minutes.

In a large metal bowl or the top of a double-boiler, whisk the eggs, egg yolks, light brown sugar, and salt until the mixture becomes pale and thick, about 2 minutes. Very slowly drizzle the hot milk mixture into the egg mixture, whisking gently but constantly.

Put the bowl over a pot of simmering water (or the bottom of a double-boiler), and cook, stirring, until the custard mixture thickens perceptibly and steams, 3 to 6 minutes. Strain the hot custard through a medium-mesh sieve—thus removing the bean pods and any bits of cooked egg—and let it cool to lukewarm. Whisk in the sour cream until no small bits of it are visible. Cover the custard and chill for at least 4 hours or overnight. The longer the custard chills, the more flavor it develops.

(If you plan to churn the ice cream at the picnic site, stop here. Simply bring the chilled peaches, custard, the remaining 1 cup cream, and Grand Marnier with you to the picnic, then proceed with the recipe. Don't forget the ice cream machine.)

When you're ready to churn the custard, stir in the peach mixture, the remaining 1 cup cream, and the Grand Marnier, if desired. Prepare the ice cream according to your ice cream maker's directions.

When the ice cream is ready, serve immediately or transfer to a freezer-safe container and freeze. The soft ice cream will become thicker in about 4 hours.

Packing reminder: Bring an ice cream scoop.

SOUR CREAM VANILLA ICE CREAM

✳ If you leave out the peaches and their sugar, this recipe makes a very luxurious and not-too-sweet vanilla ice cream. The sour cream gives it a body and nuance that sets it apart, and it's great on its own. Or you can set out an arrangement of sugared and mashed berries and fruit and let your guests top it as they please. Just follow the above recipe, ignoring anything to do with the peaches and their sugar.

STRAWBERRY-PLUM TART

✳

I t doesn't get much more summery than this—sweet, juicy plums mingling with bright strawberries and a touch of ginger and cinnamon. It makes for a pretty picture, too. The tannins in the plum skins are a nice counterpoint to the sweetness—and they also beg for a dollop of whipped cream.

MAKES ONE 9-INCH TART TO SERVE 6 TO 8

1 unbaked Five-Minute Tart Crust (page 165), fitted into
a 9-inch tart pan with a removable bottom

1 pound ripe plums (8 to 10 small to medium plums), pits removed,
cut into small segments

½ pound strawberries, stemmed and quartered

¼ cup light brown sugar

¼ cup granulated sugar

2 tablespoons unsalted butter, cut into pieces

1 tablespoon all-purpose flour

½ teaspoon vanilla extract

¼ teaspoon powdered ginger

¼ teaspoon cinnamon

Preheat the oven to 400°F. Place the tart crust on a sturdy baking sheet.

Toss all the ingredients together until everything is evenly distributed. Pour the mixture into the crust and bake the tart on the baking sheet for 40 to 50 minutes, until the filling is bubbly and the crust is browned. Serve at room temperature within 2 days.

Packing reminder: Bring a pie server.

SIMPLE YOGURT CAKE

✴

In France, *gâteau au yaourt* is a homey everyday kind of cake, made all the more charming because traditionally the empty 4-ounce (½ cup) tub of yogurt is used to measure out the ingredients for the rest of the recipe. Most yogurt in America comes in larger containers, so I've converted the recipe to standard measurements, but the easy, breezy attitude of the cake remains the same. I like to think of it as a summery kind of pound cake: a bit lighter, a bit quicker, and minus the buttery overtones.

Here I present a basic version of the cake, but it is an easy recipe to tailor to your needs. Flavor it with lemon, lime, or orange zest. Add ½ cup ground almonds or hazelnuts. Spread berries, apricots, or cherries in the middle of the batter. Drizzle it with chocolate ganache, slather it with jam, and so on and so forth.

I first learned about *gâteau au yaourt* on the website chocolate-andzucchini.com, which is one young Frenchwoman's weblog lovesong about all things edible. Check it out—there's a charming new posting and picture every day.

MAKES ONE 9-INCH CAKE TO SERVE ABOUT 8

1¼ cups all-purpose flour

2 teaspoons baking powder

1 cup sugar

½ cup plain yogurt, preferably made from whole milk

¼ cup canola oil

1 teaspoon vanilla extract

3 large eggs

Preheat the oven to 350°F. Butter a 9-inch cake pan and line the bottom with waxed paper or parchment paper.

Sift the flour and baking powder in a bowl. Separately stir together the sugar, yogurt, oil, and vanilla in another bowl and stir the eggs into it, one at a time. Stir in the flour mixture in 3 additions, just until mixed.

Pour the batter into the prepared pan and bake for 25 to 30 minutes, until the cake is slightly spongy to the touch and a toothpick comes out with a few moist crumbs on it. Let the cake cool somewhat before running a knife around the edge and turning it out on a rack to cool completely. The cake can be easily transported in its pan. It keeps well at room temperature for up to 3 days.

MY MISTAKE CAKE,
A.K.A. YOGURTLESS YOGURT CAKE

✴ That's right, during one of my tests of Simple Yogurt Cake, I forgot the—gulp—yogurt. I baked the cake anyway, and to my surprise, it was a great cake. A bit sweeter than the yogurt cake, and a bit more tender. Also, the flavor was more neutral because there was no yogurt. I make plenty of mistakes in the kitchen, but they usually don't turn into something this good.

To make My Mistake Cake, use the same technique and ingredients minus the yogurt.

GINGER-CHOCOLATE
POTS DE CRÈME

✳

Because they're baked individually in small ramekins, these simple but sublime custards are easier to transport to a picnic site than you might think. And the warmth of the ginger gives the chocolate a roundness of flavor that is absolutely breathtaking.

SERVES 6

1½-inch-long piece fresh ginger, left unpeeled

1 cup milk

⅔ cup heavy cream

3 ounces bittersweet chocolate, chopped

4 large egg yolks

¼ cup sugar

Slice the ginger into very thin rounds. Combine the milk, cream, and ginger in a saucepan and set it over high heat. When the mixture just begins to simmer, remove it from the heat, cover it, and let it steep for 1 hour.

Preheat the oven to 325°F. Line a baking dish (one large enough to accommodate six 4-ounce custard cups) with a kitchen towel.

Add the chocolate to the milk mixture and heat again, whisking gently. At the first sign of a simmer, remove the pan from the heat and continue whisking gently until all the chocolate is dissolved. This could take a few minutes.

Separately whisk the egg yolks and sugar for a minute in a bowl. Then very gradually drizzle the hot milk-cream mixture into the yolk mixture, whisking constantly but gently.

Strain the mixture though a fine-mesh strainer. Divide the custard among six 4-ounce custard cups or ramekins and arrange them in the towel-lined baking dish. Carefully add hot tap water to the baking dish so that the water comes about halfway up the sides of the cups.

Bake for 28 to 34 minutes, until the custards are set but still slightly jiggly in the center. Chill, covered, for at least 2 hours before serving.

Serve cold. They can be refrigerated for up to 3 days.

"QUICK PIC" SWEETS GALORE

✴

LEMONADE SYRUP

Pucker up, buttercup. By reducing fresh lemonade you get a sunshine yellow syrup that brings a serious zing boost to vanilla ice cream, pound cake, My Mistake Cake (page 199), and the like. Simply boil fresh lemonade (page 25) until it is reduced to less than a fourth of its original volume. The way to tell it's almost ready is that it will be quite yellow and the bubbles will sound syrupy. Does that make sense?

As the syrup cools, it will thicken to about the consistency of maple syrup. A half recipe of lemonade makes about ⅔ cup syrup. Use up your leftover lemonade like this. The syrup will keep for at least a week refrigerated, and probably much longer.

DATES STUFFED WITH ALMOND PASTE

These magical morsels are little amusements for the mouth—what the French call *amuses bouches*. Pass around a small plate of them near the end of a picnic, or let guests snap them up as appetizers. They'd go particularly well at the end of a picnic that didn't need a full dessert because the meal was rich or included a lot of fruit or sweet drinks. Get good dates from a reliable bulk foods store, natural foods store, or gourmet store.

To make them, cut lengthwise slits in several dried Medjool dates (one or two dates per person). Remove the seeds, then stuff the cavities of the dates with almond paste that has been rolled into a thin rope shape. If desired, you can roll the almond paste in shredded unsweetened coconut before stuffing it in the dates.

CHOCOLATE-DIPPED DRIED APRICOTS

Another small sweet that can't be beat. I prefer dried apricots from California. They would work well served alongside Dates Stuffed with Almond Paste (page 202).

Chop 2 ounces bittersweet chocolate and microwave it on high for 1 minute. Stir it. Then microwave it for 30-second intervals, stirring after each interval. When it's nearly melted, stir it until the residual heat melts all the chocolate. Stir in a little bit of cinnamon, to taste. Dip 8 ounces of apricots about halfway into the chocolate, and put them on a waxed-paper-lined plate or pan. Dust them with additional cinnamon, if desired. Chill the apricots and keep them cool until serving.

CINNAMON-BUTTERED SPLIT BISCUITS

My grandmother used to talk about how when she was a child growing up in the Ozarks, one of the best treats was to dip a biscuit in warm lard, then sprinkle it with sugar. I've always thought that sounded lovely, but we don't generally have hot lard sitting at the back of our stoves these days. This recipe was inspired by those legendary lard-and-sugar biscuits. These would fit in nicely at a rustic picnic or with a knapsack lunch. They *have* to be wrapped in foil. That's part of the charm, and it keeps them warm. If you have leftover biscuits, use them here.

To make 4 biscuits, combine 2 tablespoons unsalted softened butter in a bowl with 3 tablespoons confectioners' sugar and ¾ teaspoon cinnamon until smooth and uniform. Split 4 hot biscuits, such as Buttermilk Biscuits (page 110), and spread the cinnamon butter inside. Put the biscuits back together and wrap them individually in foil. Serve warm or at room temperature.

INDEX

basil:

    in corn, cucumber, et cetera, salad, 63

    in make your own spring rolls (with two sauces), 150–51

    and tomato vinaigrette, poached salmon with, 100

Beaujolais Nouveau, 31

beef:

    Cornish, pasties, 116–17

    in upside-down meatloaf, 112–13

beer:

    -boiled shrimp with dill, 138–39

    in radler, 22

beets, quick pickled, 78

berries, biscuits, honey, and cream, 156

biscuits:

    berries, honey, and cream, 156

    buttermilk, 110–11

    cinnamon-buttered split, 203

    ham, 108–9

    quickest drop, 157

black-eyed peas, in Hoppin' John, 92–93

blueberry(ies):

    in July fruit salad, 189

    -lemon custard tart, 163

blue cheese:

    crostini with peaches and, 48–49

    and walnut pesto, noodles with, 73–74

bread:

    for crostini with peaches and blue cheese, 48–49

    overnight ciabatta (bread of the ages), 89–91

breadcrumbs, in upside-down meatloaf, 112–13

Brussels sprouts, seared, 79–80

buttermilk:

    biscuits, 110–11

for in-the-pan chocolate cake, 167–68

    -peach tart, 164

cabbage, in country coleslaw, 92

cakes:

    in-the-pan chocolate, 167–68

    my mistake, a.k.a. yogurtless yogurt, 199

    simple yogurt, 198–99

Calder, Laura, 95—104

carrots, potatoes, and peas in spicy tomato sauce, 127–28

celery:

    in chicken salad with grapes, tarragon, and toasted walnuts, 70

    and green apple salad, 62

    in potato salad with horseradish and peas, 67

champagne punch #5, 23

chef's lemonade, 26

cherry(ies), sour:

    -berry pickled pineapple, 192–93

    little meatballs with, 144–45

    mini-crumbles, 158–59

chicken:

    flavorful, pieces, 140–41

    mustardy, wings, 142–43

chickpeas in intriguing tomato sauce, 77

chiffonade salad with herbs aplenty, 56–57

chives, gougères with Fontina and, 46–47

chocolate:

    -dipped dried apricots, 203

    -ginger pots de crème, 200–1

    in-the-pan, cake, 167–68

    little, cookies, 187–88

chorizo and potato tacos with *escabeche*, 152–53

garam masala popcorn, 53–54
garlic:
   double, dip, 53
   in lamb pita meze, 120–21
   in roasted potato salad with crème
      fraîche, 68–69
   in sesame noodles, 123–24
ginger:
   -chocolate pots de crème, 200–1
   iced tea, 24
   in sesame noodles, 123–24
goat's cheese:
   cherry tomatoes with minted, 35
   in cherry tomato salad, 92
   see also feta cheese
gougères with Fontina and chives,
   46–47
grapes:
   chicken salad with tarragon, toasted
      walnuts and, 70
   roasted, 39
green beans:
   couscous with hazelnuts and, 75–76
   crisp, in jalapeño oil, 83–84
   haricots verts with shallots and
      toasted pine nuts, 101
   in salade Niçoise, 60–61

ham biscuits, 108–9
hazelnuts:
   couscous with green beans and,
      75–76
   in fig pâté, 41–42
herbs, chiffonade salad with, 56
honey:
   biscuits, berries, cream and, 156
   macaroons, 160
   in spicy chai ice cream, 176–77
Hoppin' John, 92–93
horseradish:
   ham biscuits, 109

potato salad with peas and, 67
yogurt, smoked oysters with, 52

ice cream:
   perfect peach, 194–96
   sour cream vanilla, 196
   spicy chai, 176–77

Jordanian lemonade, 28
July fruit salad, 189

lamb:
   in little meatballs with cherries,
      144–45
   pita meze, 120–21
leek and pork pie, phyllo-crusted,
   146–47
lemonade:
   basic, and variations, 25–26
   chef's, 26
   Jordanian, 28
   in Pimm's, 21
   raspberry, 27
   syrup, 202
lemon-blueberry custard tart, 163
lentils, green, in vinaigrette, 93

macaroons, honey, 160
main courses:
   baked onions stuffed with fish and
      spinach, 136–37
   barbecue shredded pork, 118–19
   chorizo and potato tacos with
      escabeche, 152–53
   Cornish beef pasties, 116–17
   crepes stuffed with chard, feta, pine
      nuts, and golden raisins, 129–30
   flavorful chicken pieces, 140–41